Medical Monsters Volume One

20 Horrific Medical Serial Killers

Robert Keller

Please Leave Your Review of This Book At
http://bit.ly/kellerbooks

ISBN-13: 978-1534799240

ISBN-10: 1534799249

robertkellerauthor.com

Table of Contents

Genene Jones

On Friday, September 17, 1982, Petti McClellan brought her eight-month-old daughter, Chelsea, to the pediatric clinic in Kerrville, Texas. Chelsea was not seriously ill, but she had a cold, and having been born prematurely, with underdeveloped lungs, her mother thought it better to be safe than sorry. The Kerrville clinic had opened just a day earlier. Chelsea McClellan was it's very first patient.

While Dr. Kathleen Holland discussed Chelsea's condition with the mother, pediatric nurse, Genene Jones, took the child to another area of the clinic to play. Soon after, the nurse's cries alerted them to a problem – Chelsea had stopped breathing. Jones placed an oxygen mask over the baby's face and they rushed her to the emergency room at Sid Peterson Hospital. To everyone's relief, Chelsea recovered. It seemed that the quick-thinking Jones had saved Chelsea's life and her grateful parents were soon singing the nurse's praises around town.

Nine months later, the McClellans had cause to bring Chelsea to the clinic again, just for a routine check-up this time. Dr. Holland prescribed two standard inoculations, but shortly after nurse Jones administered the first shot, Chelsea started having difficulty breathing. It appeared that she was having a seizure, so a frantic Mrs. McClellan told the nurse to stop. Jones ignored the instruction and gave the second injection, after which the child stopped breathing altogether.

Chelsea was rushed by ambulance to Sid Peterson Hospital, with Jones cradling the baby in her arms all the way. In the ambulance, the child's breathing stalled again and her heart stopped. All attempts to revive her failed. Chelsea McClellan was pronounced dead on arrival at Sid Peterson Hospital.

Jones herself carried the child's body downstairs to the hospital morgue, sobbing hysterically. She seemed to take the death personally, but a comment made to Dr. Holland, after they'd returned to the clinic, seemed at odds with that. Jones said: "And they said there wouldn't be any excitement when we came to Kerrville."

Dr. Holland, meanwhile, was utterly bewildered by the sudden death of a seemingly healthy child. While the grief-stricken parents prepared to bury their daughter, she requested an autopsy. The results offered scant relief. Chelsea had died of SIDS, an often-fatal breathing dysfunction in babies.

One week after the funeral of Chelsea McClellan, there was a strange incident involving Genene Jones. Petti McClellan was visiting her daughter's grave at the Garden of Memories Cemetery. As she approached, she saw Jones kneeling at the grave rocking back and forth and wailing Chelsea's name over and over. Petti asked her what she was doing, but Jones gave her a blank stare and walked off without saying a word. Petti thought the behavior peculiar, but dealing with her own grief, she let it go.

Genene Jones never knew her biological parents. Born on July 13, 1950, she was immediately adopted by Dick and Gladys Jones, a wealthy couple from San Antonio, Texas. The Jones' also adopted three other children – two older and one younger than Genene. Dick Jones was a mover and shaker, a businessman and professional gambler who operated several nightclubs. He was gregarious, extravagant and generous with his money. By all accounts the Jones' doted on their adopted brood and life in the household was certainly never dull.

Despite this, Genene would later describe her childhood as unhappy. She considered herself the "black sheep" of the family and said that her parents favored the other children over her. She also felt isolated and disliked at school, mainly because she was overweight, she said. Former classmates tell a different story. They say she was aggressive, untrustworthy, bossy and manipulative, a compulsive liar who often feigned illness to get attention.

When Genene was 16, her brother and closest friend, Travis, was constructing a pipe bomb in his father's workshop when it blew up in his face, killing him instantly. Genene was devastated, but her behavior at the funeral, screaming and throwing herself to the floor, seemed contrived, designed to get attention. A year later, her father was diagnosed with terminal cancer. Dick Jones died shortly after Christmas 1967. Once again Genene's response was bizarre. She insisted to her mother that she wanted to leave school and get married immediately, in order to alleviate the pain.

Gladys Jones managed to dissuade Genene from the idea, but shortly after graduating high school, she did marry. Her husband was James "Jimmy" Delany, a high school dropout who enlisted in the navy shortly after the nuptials were completed. Left on her own for long periods, Genene began indulging her voracious sexual appetite by conducting affairs with several men, some of them married. She openly boasted about these relationships and also started spreading stories about being sexually abused as a child.

Then tragedy struck the Jones family again. Genene's older brother died of cancer. In typical self-centered fashion, she developed a morbid fear that she would contract the disease herself. At the time, she was working in a beauty salon, but she soon quit that job, convinced that she would contract cancer from the hair dyes she handled. Not long after, she enrolled on a yearlong course to become a vocational nurse.

Genene emerged with an LVN (Licensed Vocational Nurse) qualification and a burning passion for her knew vocation. Even though an LVN is at the bottom of the nursing totem she began presenting herself as an expert on all things medical. She made a habit of diagnosing friends and acquaintances on the spot, whether they asked her to or not.

By this time, Genene's marriage to Jimmy Delany had failed and she had a young child to support, with another on the way. She also had her first nursing job - at San Antonio's Methodist Hospital.

By all accounts, Genene Jones was a good nurse. But from early in her medical career there were worrying signs. After just eight months at Methodist, she was fired for making decisions in areas where she had no authority. Her next job also lasted only a few months. It seemed Jones had learned nothing from her previous problems - she was fired again, and for the same reason. Which brought her to the pediatric unit at Bexar County Medical Center. Jones would enjoy a longer tenure here - and leave a bloody imprint.

The first child to die in the care of Genene Jones did not die by her hand, but from complications after surgery to address an intestinal problem. Jones responded with an over-the-top display of grief, which her colleagues found difficult to understand. She'd hardly known the child.

But the other nurses soon learned that Jones had a desperate need for attention and that the grief was not for the dead child, but rather to garner sympathy for herself. They also realized that she wanted desperately to be needed, and would go out of her way to create little dramas that required her "personal attention." Jones also carried on her habit of overstepping her authority, sometimes overriding doctor's orders to do what she believed was right for the child.

Inevitably, this led to mistakes, many of which might have

constituted grounds for dismissal. But Jones had acquired an ally in head nurse Pat Belko, who often covered for her. With Belko to protect her, Jones grew increasingly arrogant, aggressive and foul-mouthed. She enjoyed bragging about her sexual exploits and took to bullying new nurses, more than one of whom resigned because of her.

But it was her attitude towards her young patients that upset her colleagues most. She liked making predictions about which baby would die next. If a child's health appeared to be failing, she would announce to the other nurses, "Tonight is the night." She'd become extremely excited by the emergency procedures in trying to save a child's life, then respond with extravagant grief when the patient died. She also seemed to enjoy calling the parents to let them know that their child had passed away.

And children did die, seven over one two-week period, many of them from conditions that should not have been fatal, most on the three-to-eleven shift, Genene Jones' shift, the shift other nurses called the "Death Shift."

In 1981, six-month-old Jose Antonio Flores was admitted with minor symptoms - fever, vomiting, and diarrhea. Under Jones' care, he suddenly began suffering seizures and went into cardiac arrest. Doctors fighting to save his life noticed internal bleeding and realized that his blood wasn't clotting. Still, they managed to stabilize him. Then Jones came back on duty at three the following day and Jose again went into seizure and started bleeding. Early the next morning, his little heart stopped beating. An autopsy would later indicate an overdose of heparin, an anticoagulant drug.

When a three-month-old boy developed similar symptoms, a doctor confronted Jones and asked her about the heparin in his system. She angrily denied any knowledge and stormed out. Thereafter, the child recovered and no action was taken against Jones, although stricter controls were put in place over the use of the drug.

In November 1981, the head of the pediatrics ward, Dr. James Robotham, raised concerns about Genene Jones with hospital administrators. They decided that the hospital didn't need the publicity of an inquiry and told Robotham he was overreacting.

Soon after, Joshua Sawyer, 11 months old, was brought in suffering the effects of smoke inhalation. The boy was comatose, but doctors fully expected him to recover. That is until hc suffered a heart attack and died. Lab tests showed a lethal amount of the drug Dilantin in his system, but no one saw fit to report this to the authorities. Again, Dr. Robotham asked that Jones be dismissed. Again he was ignored.

The next suspicious incident to occur at Bexar involved Rolando Santos, a one-month-old being treated for pneumonia. He suddenly started having seizures, went into cardiac arrest, and suffered extensive unexplained bleeding. When Jones was off for three days Rolando's condition improved markedly. When she returned to duty, he began hemorrhaging again and suffered another heart attack. Eventually, he lapsed into a coma. Fortunately, a doctor intervened and had him removed from the pediatric unit. The little boy then made a full recovery, and the doctor who had treated him added his voice to Robotham's, calling for an inquiry. Amazingly, the hospital still refused.

It would take the death of another child before they were forced to take action. Even then, they refused an inquiry, deciding instead that all Licensed Vocational Nurses on the pediatric unit should be replaced with higher qualified, Registered Nurses. This meant that Jones would no longer be able to care for children. She resigned in disgust. The hospital, no doubt, was glad to see her go.

It didn't take long for Genene Jones to find another job. In 1982, Dr. Kathleen Holland opened a pediatrics clinic in Kerrville, Texas. Dr. Holland had worked with Jones at Bexar County Hospital, had, in fact, stood up for her when the accusations were flying. Dr. Holland believed Jones to be a competent nurse who just needed a second chance. She employed Jones as her assistant and gave her the title, Pediatric Clinician. It was a decision she'd soon have cause to regret.

Within its first two months of operation, seven children suffered seizures at the Kerrville clinic. Kathleen Holland seemed to see nothing unusual in this disturbing pattern, but the doctors at Sid Peterson Hospital soon became suspicious, especially as the patients always recovered after receiving treatment at the hospital.

Around the time that Chelsea McClellan died, a doctor at Sid Peterson learned about the high number of infant deaths at Bexar, while Genene Jones had worked there. He brought this to the attention of a committee, and they called Dr. Holland in. They asked if she was using succinylcholine, a powerful muscle relaxant, which had been found in the blood samples of children transferred from her clinic. Dr. Holland replied that she had some, but had never used it.

Shaken by her experience, Dr. Holland returned to her office where she checked on her supply of succinylcholine. She noticed immediately that the bottles had been tampered with, the original contents extracted and replaced with saline. She confronted Jones with the evidence, but the nurse was evasive and even suggested they throw the bottle away to avoid suspicion. After Dr. Holland discovered that another bottle of succinylcholine had been ordered but was missing, she fired Jones and contacted investigators, offering her full co-operation in any inquiry.

It was already too late for her business, though. The people of Kerrville had abandoned the practice in droves and Sid Peterson hospital had suspended her privileges. Dr. Holland may have thought that she was doing a good deed by providing Jones with a job, but it had cost her livelihood, her reputation and even her marriage, as her husband initiated divorce proceedings. As a final insult, she found evidence that Jones was planning to frame her for the murders.

Genene Jones was brought to trial for the murder of Chelsea McClellan in February 1982. She was found guilty and sentenced to 99 years in prison. In November that year, she was sentenced to an additional 60 years for injuring Rolando Santos by injecting him with an undisclosed drug.

Jones will be eligible for mandatory parole in 2017, by which time she will be 66. Although suspected in the deaths of 47 more children, she was never charged with those murders.

Glennon Engleman

When we think of medical murders, the image that springs to mind is of the malevolent doctor, delivering a lethal dose of diamorphine; or the deadly nurse, dispatching her unfortunate victims with a pillow over the face or a few mils of insulin injected into an IV. Seldom do we consider the murderous dentist.

There is a reason for this. Killer dentists are a rare breed (although not unheard of – consider the high-profile cases of Drs. Sam Perera, Kenneth Taylor, and Clara Harris, for example). Dr. Glennon E. Engleman is another that fits the criteria. A dental surgeon, Dr. Engleman was also a part-time hitman, not to mention an enthusiastic murder-for-profit killer who was responsible for the deaths of at least seven people. Investigators believe he may have killed many more than that.

Glennon Engleman was born in St Louis, Missouri on February 6, 1927. He grew up in an unusual family, with a half-Cherokee mother who was heavily into astrology and convinced her children that she could travel the astral plain as a spirit. Annora Engleman also taught her offspring that it was okay to steal and commit fraud as a way of hitting back at the banks and big business.

But not all of the advice handed out by Annora was negative. Glennon was her favorite, and she encouraged him to read broadly and dedicate himself to his studies. He, initially, showed little inclination to follow her advice. Indeed, he was generally considered a troublemaker and was expelled from school several times before he eventually buckled down and set out to prove his teachers wrong. The results were quite spectacular. Not only did he graduate high school at the head of his class, he went on to college and then to dental school. Four years later, he emerged with a Doctor of Dental Medicine qualification.

Engleman was anything but your typical dentist. Setting up practice in a less than salubrious St. Louis neighborhood, he treated many of his poverty-stricken patients for free. He also developed a reputation for being homophobic, anti-Semitic, and racist. He cared so little about his personal appearance that he was often more poorly dressed than his most destitute patients. Yet he was apparently irresistible to the opposite sex. It was common knowledge that he kept a bed in his surgery for sexual trysts, and he boasted openly of fathering several children by his many lovers. He also found time to marry and divorce three different women and, if the rumors were to be believed, to carry on an incestuous relationship with his sister, Melody.

Engleman's initial foray into outright criminality involved a series of insurance frauds. First he lodged a claim against a motorboat that he had deliberately sunk, after stripping it of its engine and other expensive fittings. Then he reported a number of thefts from his home and motor vehicles. Eventually, he overstepped the mark and was arrested for fraud and sent to prison. It was a chastening experience, one that Engleman vowed never to repeat.

By 1958, Engleman was a free man again. His first wife, Ruth, had in the interim remarried, her new husband an accountant named James Bullock. One evening, Bullock set off for a class he was taking and never returned. After his wife reported him missing, he was found shot to death in his car, which was parked outside a well-known gay bar. A witness later reported seeing a man running from the area, a man who matched the description of Glennon Engleman.

As investigators started looking into the crime, they turned up one interesting detail. It appeared that Engleman and his former wife were still involved intimately. Engleman was therefore pulled in for questioning and provided an alibi, which turned out to be a lie. The investigators must have thought that they had him, but the quick thinking dentist concocted another story. He admitted to lying about his whereabouts but said that he'd done so to cover the fact that he'd actually been performing an illegal abortion. Unable to prove otherwise, the police were forced to let him go. As for the abortion charge, Engleman refused to name names, and with no witnesses to testify against him, that charge was also dropped.

Shortly after, Ruth Bullock cashed a $64,000 policy on her husband's life. $20,000 of that money went directly to Engleman.

Five years passed. In 1963, Glennon Engleman was still running his rather unconventional dental practice and still chasing the ladies. His latest conquest was an attractive 18-year-old named Sandy, who enjoyed hanging around the drag strip Engleman had recently invested in. Sandy was besotted with Engleman, so when he roped her in to participate in a murder-for-profit scheme, she readily agreed. The plan was for Sandy to seduce a young man named Eric Frey, a wannabe drag racer who enjoyed hanging around the strip. She would then marry Frey and take out insurance on his life. The rest would be left to Engleman. He'd ensure that Frey met with an "accident." He and Sandy would then split the proceeds of the insurance policy.

Eric and Sandy were duly married and took out policies on each other's lives. On the evening of September 26, 1963, Engleman invited Frey and some other friends out to the drag strip. Once there, he told them that he planned on dynamiting an old well, as he was afraid that someone might fall down it. He asked Frey to help and the two walked off into the darkness.

Moments later, several of those present heard Frey cry out. Engleman had clubbed him over the head with a rock and pushed him into the well. Then, as the critically injured young man lay in the few inches of muddy water at the bottom, Engleman climbed down and drowned him. He then dynamited the well before calling the police. His story, that Frey had accidently blown himself up, was believed. Sandy received a $25,000 payout, $16,000 of which found its way to Engleman.

1963 was also the year that Glennon Engleman met the man who would become a partner in his murderous schemes. Like

Engleman, Robert Handy was a much-divorced ladies man with an eye for easy money. The two met after Handy, a carpenter, did some work for Engleman's brother. Thereafter they became firm friends, with Handy totally in awe of his new buddy. A year after their initial meeting, Handy was arrested due to a counterfeit operation he and Engleman had been running. Despite the offer of a reduced sentence, he refused to give Engleman up and did his jail time alone.

Hardy was released in 1968. In 1975, he and Engleman were again looking for a score. Burned by his failed counterfeiting operation, Engleman decided to fall back on the method he knew best. This time, he roped in Carmen Miranda, a 24-year-old dental nurse at his practice. Engleman had known Carmen since she was a child and he had helped her impoverished family through some tough times. She was willing to do just about anything for him. What he wanted her to do was marry a man named Peter Halm.

The story then followed a familiar path. Carmen married her man and took out a policy on his life. In September 1976, Engleman instructed her to bring Halm to a picnic spot, in an area popular with hunters. There, Engleman and Handy waited, concealed in bushes, Engleman armed with a rifle. As the couple approached, Engleman drew a bead on Halm's head and fired, killing him instantly. The death was ruled a shooting accident. Engleman profited to the tune of $10,000.

But Engleman's new windfall was short-lived. Most of it, in fact, went to the IRS in back taxes. Within a year, he was looking for another score.

Engleman's latest accomplice was a divorcee named Barbara, with whom he'd been having an affair. Following his usual M.O. he persuaded Barbara to find a husband, someone who he insisted should not be a high-profile person or a law enforcement officer, as the death of such an individual would attract too much attention. Barbara duly obliged, seducing and marrying a man named Ronald Gusewelle.

Shortly after the nuptials were completed, Barbara contacted Engleman with a surprising piece of news. It appeared that Ronald's parents were well-off farmers and that he was due to inherit half a million dollars on their deaths. Ever the opportunist, Engleman decided there and then to cash in on this fortuitous piece of intelligence.

On the evening of November 3, 1988, Engleman and Handy drove to the Gusewelle farmhouse. Handy remained in the car while Engleman knocked on the door and was allowed in, after claiming to be a representative of the Farm Bureau. Once inside, he produced a gun and instructed 71-year-old Arthur Gusewelle and his 55-year-old wife, Vernita, to lie face down on the floor. He then cold-bloodedly shot both victims in the back of the head before he and Handy ransacked the house and then fled.

Engleman thought that he had killed both victims, but Arthur Gusewelle survived long enough to drag himself to the phone and call the police. He died later that night, leaving his son Ronald a much wealthier man.

The murder of the Gusewelle's was believed by police to be a hold-up gone wrong, which was exactly what Engleman had intended. Now all he had to do was wait, before executing the second part of his plan. By March 1979, he figured that enough time had passed. The estate had in the interim been settled and Barbara had taken out $193,000 in life insurance on her husband's life. This was going to be Glennon Engleman's biggest score.

On March 14, 1979, Engleman and Handy arrived at the Gusewelle residence. Barbara ushered them into the garage where they hid while waiting for Ronald Gusewelle to arrive home. When he did, Engleman shot him once in the chest before bludgeoning him to death with a hammer (he'd later claim that it was Handy who did the bludgeoning).

With Gusewelle dead, Engleman and Handy crammed him into the trunk of his car and drove him to an area commonly frequented by prostitutes. Their hope was that the police would believe that he'd been killed as the result of a sexual transaction turned sour and that was exactly how it played out. Barbara Gusewelle was now a very wealthy woman and a substantial portion of that wealth flowed to Engleman.

But Engleman had other problems to contend with. He was involved in a legal dispute with a dental technician named Sophie Marie Berrera who had done some impression work for his surgery and had gone unpaid. Berrera then decided to take legal action on the matter, filing a claim for $14,500. It was a fatal mistake when dealing with a man like Glennon Engleman.

On January 14, 1980, Sophie Berrera got into her car and turned the key. She was killed instantly by an explosion that blew off both of her feet and caused severe trauma to her internal organs.

But Engleman had erred badly in straying from his usual M.O. It was well known that he and Berrera were involved in a legal dispute. In fact, family members told the police that Sophie had firmly believed Engleman was trying to kill her. She'd even found an undetonated bomb in her garage.

With a suspect now in their sights, the police began looking into Engleman's background and quickly discovered that he had benefitted from two life insurance policies involving suspicious deaths. They began talking to Engleman's friends and family, but no one was giving anything up until they tracked down Engleman's third wife (who, like his first, was named Ruth).

Ruth was, at first, reluctant to speak to the police. Despite her divorce from Engleman, she was still involved sexually with him. She was also well aware of what he was capable of. But under gentle probing she eventually started opening up, first telling police about the frauds she'd helped Engleman pull off, then getting on to the murders he had committed. Afraid that Engelman was planning to kill her, she agreed to wear a wire and to try and coax Engleman into an admission of guilt.

That proved to be easier than expected. Engleman enjoyed boasting about his crimes and it did not take much encouragement before he was sounding off about the murder he'd committed on behalf of his dental nurse, Carmen Miranda. The audio of that conversation found its way into the hands of the authorities, earning the former Ruth Engleman a placement in the federal witness protection program.

Glennon Engleman and Robert Handy were arrested in February 1980, along with Carmen Miranda and her brother, Nick. The Mirandas were later granted immunity in exchange for their testimony against Engleman. Handy also turned on his old buddy in exchange for a lesser sentence, although he remained devoted to Engleman and wrote him a series of fawning letters, apologizing for his actions.

It all added up to a powerful case against the murderous dentist, but it would take several trials before prosecutors were able to secure convictions for all the crimes he stood accused of. He was sentenced to three terms of life imprisonment and died in prison on March 3, 1999.

As for Engleman's confederates, Robert Handy was sentenced to 17 years, while Barbara Gusewelle received a prison term of 50 years for her part in her husband's murder.

Colin Norris

Colin Norris was born in Glasgow, Scotland on February 12, 1976, and raised in the Glasgow suburb of Partick. His childhood was, by all accounts, a happy one, with a close nuclear family. He was an active child, a Boy Scout and a keen participant in amateur dramatics. He participated in a project to help learning disabled people and was considered polite and well behaved.

But all of that was to change in 1983 when his parents separated. Colin, just seven years old at the time, remained with his mother and when the divorce was finalised two years later, she gained custody. After that, the boy's academic performance, never stellar to begin with, suffered. He left school at sixteen and enrolled on a course of study to qualify as a travel agent.

Norris had seen very little of his father since the divorce and while the two were not estranged exactly, their relationship had never been close. But in 1992, an event occurred which was to drive a wedge between them. It also provides a valuable insight into the character of Colin Norris. While attending a family funeral, Norris was caught red-handed stealing money from the handbags of his elderly relatives. Disgusted by his actions, Norris' father broke off all contact.

By 1998, Norris had been working in the travel industry for six years and was bored with the vocation. He started casting around for a new career path, something (as he told friends) that would make a difference. He eventually struck on the idea of training to be a nurse.

Given Norris' personality, it appears a strange choice. By now openly gay, Norris had grown into a vain and narcissistic young man with a highly elevated opinion of his own abilities and a deeply engrained argumentative streak. Still, in September 1998, he registered at Dundee University's School of Nursing and Midwifery and began studying towards the Higher Nursing Diploma.

It wasn't long before there was conflict. Norris clashed frequently with his tutors, in fact, with anyone in authority. He appeared always to think he knew better and was loathe to take instruction from anyone. His fellow students differed in their assessment of him. Some described him as extremely self-confident; others were probably more accurate when they called him smug and conceited.

In January 1999, Norris attended a series of lectures that would sow the seeds for the monster he would become. The subject was diabetes, standard enough matter for a medical trainee. But Norris appeared particularly interested in the lecturer's comments on the misuse of insulin and how one particular nurse had used the drug to murder several of her elderly patients.

Norris was by now at the stage of his training where practical work dominated the curriculum. In May 1999, he served an internship at Dundee's Ninewells Hospital. Later that year, he spent time working at the Royal Victoria Hospital, also in Dundee. At both of these institutions he received further training in diabetic care, mostly attending geriatric patients. Norris hated working with the elderly and wasn't slow to let his tutors know about it. During this time, his work attendance suddenly deteriorated as he took time off for any minor ailment, including several weeks with a "sore throat."

Notwithstanding his poor attitude, and worse attendance record, Colin Norris was awarded the Higher Nursing Diploma in June 2001. A couple of months later, he landed his first nursing job, as a staff nurse at Leeds General Infirmary in Leeds, Yorkshire. Such was the demand for qualified nurses that he also worked at a second hospice in the city, St James Hospital.

Colin Norris was a junior nurse, lowest on the caregiver totem pole. But you'd never know it from his attitude. He soon gained a reputation for being difficult, ready to challenge anyone in authority. He particularly disliked the menial tasks assigned to him. Someone with his qualifications should be put to more meaningful work than changing bedpans and mopping up vomit, he'd tell anyone who was prepared to listen. And he'd often take out his frustrations on the patients. He refused, on one occasion to help an elderly man who had fallen out of bed. Another time, he refused to remove a catheter for a patient, telling him to do it himself. When other patients protested, he told them to "rot in hell."

If the hospital authorities got to hear of any of these incidents, they took no action against Norris. And despite it being common knowledge on the wards that he hated elderly patients, he remained assigned to their care. Being gay, Norris found it particularly repulsive caring for elderly women. The job he hated most was performing bed baths on women, many of who were suffering from incontinence.

One might ask why Norris persevered in a job that he so clearly hated, why he didn't just quit or at least ask for a transfer to another department. But that question fails to take into account Norris' narcissistic personality. He'd worked very hard to earn his diploma and wasn't about to walk away. If anyone were going to leave, it would be the patients.

On May 2, 2001, 90-year-old Vera Wilby was admitted to Leeds General after suffering a broken hip in a fall. Doctors managed to reset the hip and Mrs. Wilby appeared to be recovering well. But then her condition suddenly began to deteriorate and she eventually lapsed into a semi-conscious state. Doctors were able to intervene and save her life although they remained puzzled as to what had caused the episode in the first place. It would later be determined that someone had tried to overdose her with morphine. That revelation, unfortunately, would only come after four other elderly women had died.

A month after the attempt on Vera Wilby's life, 80-year-old Doris Ludlam was admitted to the same ward, also suffering from a broken hip. This was, of course, the ward where Colin Norris worked and he was one of the nurses assigned to her care. On June 25, 2002, Mrs. Ludlam was found in a comatose state and despite the best efforts of medical staff, she died two days later. Tests would later determine that she'd been given a massive dose of diamorphine, followed by a shot of insulin.

Norris was not in attendance when Doris Ludlam was discovered, as he'd just completed his shift. With the next victim, however, it was he who raised the alarm. Bridget Bourke, aged 88, had recently suffered a stroke. On July 21, Norris reported that he'd found Mrs. Bourke unconscious. She died the following day and tests would show that she had extremely low blood sugar levels.

Doris Ludlam and Bridget Bourke had both died at Leeds General, the other common denominator being that Colin Norris was one of the attending nurses. And Norris was again in attendance at the death of the next victim, although she died at Norris' "second job," at St. James Hospital. Irene Crookes, 79, had been admitted with a fractured hip and breathing difficulties. She died on October 20, having lapsed into a hypoglycemic coma.

So far, Norris had gotten away with three murders and in typical serial killer fashion he was getting overconfident. When 86-year-old Ethel Hall was checked into his ward on November 14, he told another nurse that he was worried about her health. The nurse was surprised. Mrs. Hall had undergone successful hip surgery and appeared to be recovering well. She was even walking around the ward with the help of a cane. Norris though was insistent, telling his colleague: "Whenever I do nights, someone always dies."

Six days later, on November 20, Norris' concern was validated when Ethel Hall was found in the early hours of the morning, struggling for breath. Tests showed that her blood sugar was abnormally low, her insulin levels extremely elevated. It was a condition that could not have occurred naturally. Faced with the prospect of a killer on the wards, hospital administrators called in the police.

Ethel Hall would eventually die on December 11, 2002. By then, West Yorkshire Police had already begun their interrogation of doctors and nurses at Leeds General. Their attention quickly zeroed in on Colin Norris after they learned of his comments regarding Mrs. Hall's health. But Norris proved a wily adversary for his interrogators. He admitted that he'd had "a lot of bad luck" with patients dying on his shift, but insisted that he had nothing to do with their deaths. It would be over two years before investigators built a strong enough case to charge him with murder.

Colin Norris went on trial at Newcastle Crown Court on October 16, 2005, charged with four counts of murder and one of attempted murder. Convicted on all charges he was sentenced to life in prison, with at least 30 years to be served before he is considered for parole.

Michael Swango

Southern Illinois University (SUI) is one of the state's most revered higher learning institutions. It accepts only the best and the brightest and Michael Swango certainly met that criteria. And yet, he was decidedly different from his peers. Classmates interviewed after Swango had entered the halls of infamy, recalled that he spent more time working as a part-time ambulance attendant than at his studies. They also remembered some strange behavior on his part. Despite the high marks he regularly earned on written exams, he was sloppy at practical work. On one occasion he had difficulty identifying the position of the human heart on an x-ray. On another, he so badly botched the dissection of a cadaver that his efforts became a school joke. Then there was his habit of dropping to the floor to perform a set of military-style push-ups whenever he failed to correctly answer a question from one of his instructors.

Swango also seemed to have a morbid fascination with critically ill patients. When they eventually succumbed, he took obvious relish in scrawling 'DIED' across their charts in big red letters. And many of the patients that Swango attended, did die. So many, in fact, that the other students began calling him "Double-O Swango" – a parody of James Bond 007 and his license to kill.

Michael Swango was born Joseph Michael Swango in Tacoma, Washington on October 21, 1954, and raised in Quincy, Illinois. From an early age, he insisted on being called Michael or Mike. He was a well-behaved child, an honor student, and a talented musician, playing clarinet with the Christian Brothers High School Marching Band. After graduating valedictorian in 1972, he enrolled at Millikin University College to pursue a degree in music.

Then, during his sophomore year, everything changed. Swango suddenly began dressing in military fatigues, even painting his car a military green. He developed a macabre fascination with violent and tragic events and started collecting a scrapbook of newspaper cuttings featuring automobile and airplane crashes, military coups, murders, arson, and riots. He began neglecting his studies, eventually dropping out and enlisting in the Marine Corps.

Swango's mother Muriel was distressed at his decision having spent much of her life as a lonely military wife while her husband Colonel Virgil Swango completed various tours of duty. But if Muriel feared that Michael would follow a similar path, that fear was soon put to rest. Michael completed just one stint in the Marines before being honorably discharged in 1976. To the delight of his mother, he announced that he intended studying medicine.

Swango enrolled at Quincy College, where he majored in both Biology and Chemistry. He also began working as an ambulance attendant at a local medical center. Despite this extra-curricula activity cutting into his study time, he maintained an A average. He graduated summa cum laude, elevating his name to the top of Southern Illinois University's long waiting list of prospective pre-med students.

In 1982, while Swango was in his last year at SIU, his father died. After the funeral, his mother presented him with something she'd found among the colonel's personal effects. It was a scrapbook, very similar to the one Michael himself had been compiling, a catalog of mayhem and bloody disasters.

Inspired by the book, Swango began working feverishly on expanding his own collection. When an acquaintance asked him about his strange hobby, Swango allegedly answered: “If I'm ever accused of murder, this will prove that I'm mentally unstable.”

Swango should have graduated in June 1982, but by now he was spending so much time at the ambulance service that he began to take short cuts in his all-important practical work. He often showed up late or snuck out early. When one of his professors caught him filling out a patient’s chart despite not having bothered to examine her, Swango was in deep trouble. Faced with the possibility of expulsion, Swango hired an attorney and a compromise was reached. Swango was not expelled, but he was required to repeat the work he'd fudged. And there was another price to pay, the offer of an internship with the University of Iowa's neurosurgery department was suddenly withdrawn.

This setback was soon forgotten. By the time Swango received his diploma in April 1983, he had been offered a yearlong internship at Ohio State University Medical Center, to be followed by a residency position in its neurosurgery department.

The OSU Medical Center, located in Columbus, Ohio, is a prestigious institution attracting only the best pre-med graduates, so it didn't take long for Swango's shortcomings to become apparent. The doctor overseeing Swango's work complained about his general ineptitude and uncaring manner with patients. Fellow interns spoke of his strange behavior and his preoccupation with the Nazi genocide of the Jews.

Then, on the morning of January 31, 1984, the hospital had something more serious to concern itself with than Swango's odd behavior. At about 10 a.m. on that day, Swango entered the room of a neurosurgery patient named Ruth Barrick. He told the attending nurse, Deborah Kennedy, that he wanted to check on the IV hook-up. Kennedy found this strange as such calls were normally done earlier, and usually by a doctor, not an intern. But she left the room when instructed to do so. She returned some twenty minutes later to find Swango gone and the patient in obvious distress. Ruth Barrick was writhing in pain, turning blue. She appeared to be suffocating. Doctors rushed to resuscitate her and she later recovered in the Intensive Care Unit. But the attending physicians were puzzled as to what had caused an obvious respiratory failure.

A week later, on February 6, Nurse Anne Ritchie observed a low reading on Barrick's IV tube. She called a doctor to check it. Swango answered the call, spending an unusually long time at the task. When he eventually left, Ritchie returned to check on the patient and found Ruth Barrick gasping for air, her skin a ghastly shade of blue. Despite emergency treatment, Barrick died.

At around 9 p.m. the following evening, student nurse Karolyn Beery saw Swango inject something into the IV of an elderly patient, Rena Cooper. Moments later, Cooper began shaking violently, struggling for air, her complexion turning blue. Resuscitation efforts, fortunately, saved her life. Although unable to speak, Cooper motioned for a notebook and pencil. A former nurse herself, she wrote: "Someone gave me some med in my IV and paralyzed all of me, lungs, heart, speech."

The following morning, Cooper's attending doctor asked her to describe the person who had tampered with her IV. Her description - and that of Nurse Beery - perfectly fit Swango. However, when confronted with the allegation he angrily denied any involvement.

The nurses on the ward were unconvinced. They began comparing notes and soon discovered an alarmingly high number of deaths in that area since Swango's appointment - more in a few weeks than there had been in the previous year. Besides Ruth Barrick, there had been six others, all of whom had appeared to be recovering well until Swango arrived on the scene.

The nurses took their concerns to Assistant Director of Nursing Jan Dickson, who escalated them to Neurosurgery Professor Joseph Goodman. To their surprise, Goodman responded unsympathetically, suggesting that the nurses should focus more on their jobs and less on feeding the rumor mill. Nonetheless, an investigation of sorts was conducted. It cleared Swango of any wrongdoing and reinstated him to full intern privileges, although he was transferred to another part of the hospital. No sooner had he started work there, than a number of unexplained deaths began to occur.

On February 19, 1984, Charlotte Warner, 72, was found dead in her room. She'd just recovered from surgery and had been doing well. Yet something had suddenly caused her blood to clot in several organs.

That same day, Evelyn Pereney began bleeding profusely from body orifices, shortly after being examined by Dr. Swango.

On February 20, Swango entered the room of Anna Mae Popko, 22. Anna Mae's mother was visiting her at the time, but Swango instructed her to leave the room, as he needed to give Anna an injection (to increase her blood pressure, he said). After a brief argument, Mrs. Popko relented. Not long afterward, Swango walked from the room. "She's dead now," he told Mrs. Popko. "You can go look at her."

Swango again avoided official action, but his reputation would impact his tenure at OSU. In late February, a review board met to decide whether he had a future as a resident doctor at the hospital. The outcome was a unanimous no, but it was not the suspicious deaths that were Swango's downfall, rather it was his poor work performance. Angered by this rejection, Swango left Ohio and returned to his hometown of Quincy, Illinois.

Swango soon got a job as a paramedic with the Adams County Ambulance Corps. His new employers were no doubt delighted to land someone of his qualifications and medical expertise, but Swango's new work colleagues saw a different side to him. He hadn't been working there long when he admitted that violence turned him on and that his main reason for becoming a paramedic was to surround himself with the mayhem and bloodshed that are part of the job.

On another occasion, he described to them his ultimate fantasy. "Picture a school bus crammed with kids, smashing head-on with a trailer truck loaded down with gasoline. We're summoned. We get there in a jiffy just as another gasoline truck rams the bus. Up in flames it goes! Kids are hurled through the air, everywhere, on telephone poles, on the street, especially along an old barbed wire fence along the road. All burning."

Swango's fellow corpsmen, in the main, accepted his quirks and regarded such outpourings as black humor. That is, until the donut incident.

It was customary for members of the corps to take turns bringing treats for others to share. When it was Swango's turn, he delighted his co-workers by bringing in an assortment of freshly baked donuts. However, within hours of consuming the treats, every man on the crew had to be sent home after suffering from stomach cramps, nausea, dizziness, and vomiting. Everyone, that is, except Swango.

Later, when the paramedics realized that Swango hadn't eaten any of the donuts, they angrily confronted him. He vehemently denied any wrongdoing. The following evening, Swango and a colleague were assigned to routine emergency detail at a high school football game. At halftime, Swango offered to buy his colleague a soda. After drinking just half of the cup, the man became violently ill. He would spend three days in bed recovering from his symptoms – cramping, headaches, and nausea.

Swango was again the main suspect even if no one could prove any wrongdoing. Nonetheless, his colleagues decided to launch their own investigation. While Swango was out on a call, they opened his locker. Inside they found a box of arsenic-based ant poison. They decided to set a trap.

A pot of iced tea was brewed and left on the counter, where they knew Swango would have access to it. Once Swango went out, they poured the liquid from the pot into another container and brought it to the local coroner, who sent it to the FBI lab for testing. Results indicated traces of arsenic. Swango was promptly arrested and charged with seven counts of aggravated battery.

Swango's trial opened at the Quincy Courthouse on April 22, 1985. Despite his protestations of innocence he was found guilty and sentenced to a five-year term, to be served at Centralia Correctional Center. While in prison, Swango granted an interview to John Stossel of the TV program 20/20. It was a move that would come back to haunt him.

By the time of his release, on August 21, 1987, the furor over Swango's arrest had died down, but he decided it was probably better if he left Illinois to avoid local gossip. He moved to Newport News, Virginia, and promptly applied for a license to practice medicine in that state. He was turned down.

Unable to work as a doctor, Swango found a job as a counselor at the state's Career Development Center, then as a lab technician at coal exporter Aticoal Services. While he was employed at the company, several Aticoal employees fell ill and almost died from food poisoning. However, Swango's history as a poisoner was unknown in these parts and no suspicion fell on him.

In 1991, Swango was taking a refresher course at Newport News' Riverside Hospital when he met Kristin Kinney, a beautiful, 26-year-old nurse who had recently divorced. Kristin was engaged when they first met, but as her friendship with Swango blossomed, she broke off the engagement and the two of them became romantically involved.

By this time, Swango was desperate to get back into medical practice and had sent applications to a number of facilities across the country. In September 1991, one of them finally responded. Dr. Anthony Salem, director of the University of South Dakota in Sioux Falls was impressed by Swango's resume. Before inviting him for an interview, though, he needed to clarify one or two points, most importantly the battery conviction in Illinois. Swango spun him a story about a barroom brawl for which he'd taken the fall. Salem was impressed by his frankness and invited him to Sioux Falls for an interview.

On October 3, Swango faced a panel of several teaching doctors. Incredibly, none of them asked about the battery conviction. Neither did anyone bother checking out Swango's version of events with the authorities.

In March 1992, Swango got the news he'd been waiting for. His application had been accepted, his residency to begin in June. He immediately proposed to Kristen and after she accepted they began planning their move to Sioux Falls, where she'd secured a position at Royal C. Johnson Veterans' Memorial Hospital.

The couple soon settled into their new life, and for once Swango seemed determined to make a success of his medical career. He quickly gained a reputation as an excellent ER doctor. Meanwhile, Kristin became a valued and well-liked member of staff at the VA hospital. Things were finally looking up for Michael Swango and it was perhaps for that reason that he became overconfident.

In October 1992, despite being an unlicensed doctor who had obtained an internship under false pretenses, Swango applied for membership of the American Medical Association (AMA). He probably counted on them not checking his credentials. If that was the case, he was wrong. While conducting its usual background checks, the AMA discovered the true reason for Swango's battery conviction. As chance would have it, this discovery coincided with 20/20's re-broadcast of the 1986 prison interview reporter John Stossel had done with Swango.

The effect of this double blow was devastating. Swango was fired from his job and he and Kristen found themselves inundated by reporters. Swango cursed and threatened lawsuits and insisted that he'd been railroaded, but the proof was there for all to see, in his own words. Kristen began suffering severe headaches and although she believed that it was due to stress, she couldn't help but wonder if Swango was putting something into her food. Eventually, she couldn't take it any longer and returned to her parents' home in Virginia.

Once she was away from Swango, the headaches abruptly stopped. But she continued to love him, perhaps convincing herself that Swango was innocent, that he had been set up, as he claimed. What she couldn't explain away was the headaches and how they'd stopped right after she'd left him. As a trained nurse, she understood the implication. It was more than she could bear. In June 1993, Kristen Kinney took her own life.

Her suicide note was written to her mother and stepfather, but there was an

addendum below, addressed to Swango. It read:

"I love you more! You're the most precious man I've ever known - Love, KK."

Swango, meanwhile, was in New York State where he'd amazingly secured another medical position, this time with the University of New York Stony Brook Medical School. The barroom brawl story had come up trumps for him again.

Swango's first assignment was at the Veterans' Administration complex in Northport, Long Island, beginning on July 1. That first evening, Dominic Buffalino, mysteriously died within hours of Swango taking charge of his case. It would be the first of many such occurrences over the next few months. Aldo Serinei, Thomas Sammarco, and George Siano all succumbed to mysterious symptoms shortly after being attended by Michael Swango.

And then there was the case of Barron Harris, an elderly patient who'd been admitted to the hospital after contracting pneumonia. One evening, Barron's wife, Elsie, found Swango giving him a shot. "Vitamins," Swango explained when she asked. But within days, Harris' condition faltered. Soon he slipped into a coma from which he never recovered. Elsie Harris sued the hospital for negligence. The case was thrown out of court for lack of evidence.

But while Swango may have dodged a bullet, his past was about to catch up with him again. Kristin Kinney's parents were finding it difficult to cope with their daughter's suicide. Mostly they were angry that Swango, who they felt was responsible, had not faced any action for his deceit.

Then a chance conversation with one of KrIsten's friends led to them discovering that Swango was practicing medicine again. A call was placed to Dr. Jordan Cohen, Dean of Stony Brook. In short order Swango's residency was terminated. But not before the press got wind of the story. Swango found himself in the midst of another media storm and questions began to be raised about the mysterious deaths at Stony Brook.

As the Justice Department launched an investigation, Swango dropped from sight. In mid-1994, he was tracked to Atlanta, Georgia. But no sooner had the FBI put him under surveillance than he disappeared again and, this time, there was no trace of him.

The FBI believed that he'd either killed himself or left the country and they were right in the second assumption. Swango had absconded to the southern African country of Zimbabwe. Here he found work at the Lutheran mission hospital in the remote village of Mnene.

After completing a five-month internship at Mpilo Hospital in Bulawayo to familiarize himself with local conditions, Swango was ready to take up his new post. He proved an able and hardworking physician, often putting in extra hours to improve conditions and procedures at Mnene. But soon enough, his enthusiasm began to wane. He became surly and there were complaints about his attitude towards the nuns and other employees. And then patients began to die.

The first was Rhoda Mahlamvana who entered the hospital with burns suffered in a house fire. She was recovering well until Swango took charge of her case. Then her condition began to deteriorate and she died soon after.

Others followed. Katazo Shava died after accusing Swango of injecting him with “something bad.” Phillimon Chipoko succumbed after a foot amputation. Virginia Sibanda nearly died during childbirth, with Swango in attendance. She later told a nun that

Swango had injected her with a needle he'd withdrawn from his lab coat. When Margaret Zhou died after a minor procedure, the nuns at Mnene had had enough. They approached the hospital's director, Dr. Zshiri, and insisted that he call in the police.

A search warrant was obtained for Swango's cottage and turned up a huge cache of drugs and medical equipment as well as bottles and tins of substances foreign to the Zimbabwe doctors. Swango was outraged at the intrusion and the charges now levied against him. He hired one of Zimbabwe's top lawyers, David Coltart, to defend him. Yet, as the evidence against him continued to build, Swango suddenly disappeared.

He hid out in Zambia, then Europe, for almost a year, before returning to the United States, where he was arrested at Chicago's O'Hare Airport on June 27, 1997. Charged with practicing medicine without a license, he was escorted to New York for trial. In the meanwhile, the FBI was building a murder case against him.

Swango was eventually charged with the murders of Thomas Sammarco, Aldo Serinei, and George Siano all of whom had died at the VA Hospital in Long Island. He was also charged with the battery of Barron Harris. A further murder charge followed, for the death of 19-year-old Cynthia McGee, who Swango had injected with potassium while he was an intern at Ohio State University Hospital.

Facing a possible death sentence, Swango came clean and admitted to murdering the three patients at the veterans' hospital. He was sentenced to life in prison without parole. He later received an additional life sentence for the murder of Cynthia McGee. But this is likely to be just the tip of the iceberg. The FBI believes that Dr. Michael Swango may have committed as many as 60 murders.

Gwendolyn Graham & Cathy Wood

It started as a game, a sick pact by lesbian lovers to kill patients at the hospital where they worked. By the time it was over, five frail, elderly women would be dead, killed for no other reason than to satisfy the sexual fantasies of a pair of reprobates named Gwendolyn Graham and Cathy Wood.

Gwendolyn Graham was born in California on August 6, 1963, and raised in Tyler, Texas. Growing up, she was a quiet and respectful child who kept mostly to herself and seldom smiled. She'd later claim that this was due to the sexual abuse she suffered at the hands of her father. Whether that is true or not, Graham left home as soon as she was able, drifting for a while before ending up in Michigan in 1986. There she found work as a nurse's aide at the Alpine Manor Nursing Home in Walker, a suburb of Grand Rapids.

Graham's immediate supervisor at Alpine Manor was Cathy Wood. Horribly obese at over 400 pounds, the 24-year-old had recently divorced, ending her seven-year marriage. She was alone and friendless in the world, so when Graham started paying her attention, a friendship quickly developed. Before long, that friendship had evolved into a sexual relationship, with Graham the dominant partner. She introduced Wood to the local gay scene, parties, and casual sex. Wood, though, was devoted to Graham and prepared to do just about anything her lover asked.

And Gwen Graham asked a lot. She was heavily into sexual asphyxia and enjoyed throttling and suffocating Cathy during their lovemaking. Sometimes she'd even force a pillow over her lover's face and hold it there until she blacked out. If Cathy Wood had any complaints, she didn't voice them.

Neither, apparently, did Cathy raise any objections when Gwen suggested murdering elderly patients as part of their sex play. Her original idea was to target patients with the initials M-U-R-D-E-R, spelling out the word Murder, a sort of sick in-joke between them. But the first victim she chose fought so vigorously that Graham was forced to abandon the attack. Two more botched attempts occurred in December 1986 before Graham had to concede that her plan wasn't going to work. From now on, she would target the weakest of victims, those who were incapable of fighting back.

First, though, there were some anxious days for the lovers to endure. They were certain that the three women Graham had attacked would report them, that they'd be hauled before a disciplinary committee and fired, maybe even arrested. Yet, amazingly, none of the victims complained. It was a narrow escape, one that buoyed them for the diabolical murder spree they were about to carry out.

In January 1987, Graham posted Wood as a lookout and entered the room of an Alzheimer's patient. She approached the bed holding a damp washcloth, which she placed over the victim's mouth and nose, holding it down until the woman stopped breathing. Wood, standing in the doorway, witnessed the entire attack. Afterward, the two were so overcome with excitement that they retired to an empty room and had sex.

Over the three months that followed, four more elderly women would fall prey to the heartless killers. Given the frail condition of the victims, the deaths were ruled natural and raised no alarm bells. Perhaps annoyed that they weren't getting "credit" Graham and Wood began bragging about the murders, even showing off the souvenirs they'd taken from their victims – an ankle bracelet, a handkerchief, a broach, a set of dentures. It was an audacious risk, but one they were willing to take because talking about the murders excited them. Unfortunately, the colleagues they confided in took the boasts to be a sick joke and didn't report them to the authorities.

How long Graham and Wood might have continued on their murderous path and how many more victims they might have claimed, is open to conjecture. But, by April 1987, a rift had opened up between the lovers. Graham wanted Wood to play a more active role in the next murder, but Wood baulked at the idea. Graham then insisted that Wood should kill the next victim in order to "prove her love," but Wood refused. A short while later,

Graham found a new lover and quit her job. She moved back to Texas, leaving Wood in the lurch and heartbroken.

Wood was distraught at her abandonment, but she and Graham still spoke regularly on the phone. After Graham found a new nursing job, at the Mother Frances Children's Hospital in Tyler, Texas, Wood began to worry that she might start harming the infants under her care. When Graham confessed her desire to "take one of the babies and smash it up against a window," Wood decided to act. She contacted her ex-husband and told him she needed to talk.

Ken Wood, however, was unconvinced by his former wife's confession to the five Alpine Manor murders. He was certain that she was just looking for attention and decided to sit on the information. It would be fourteen months before he eventually contacted the police in October 1988.

But even the Grand Rapids police had difficulty believing the story of wholesale slaughter on the wards. They did, however, have a responsibility to investigate and began looking into the 40 patient deaths that had occurred at Alpine Manor during the first quarter of 1987. All had been attributed to natural causes, but on reflection eight looked suspicious. Detectives eventually ruled out three of those and honed in on the deaths of 60-year-old Marguerite Chambers, Edith Cole, 89, Myrtle Luce, 95, 79-year-old Mae Mason, and 74-year-old Belle Burkhard.

Although there was no forensic evidence of murder in any of these cases, Ken Wood's statement, and the testimony of nurses at

Alpine Manor, led eventually to the arrest of Graham and Wood in December 1988.

Gwendolyn Graham was extradited to Michigan in September 1989. In the interim, Cathy Wood had entered into a plea agreement, accepting charges of second-degree murder in order to avoid a life sentence. She emerged at the trial as the star prosecution witness, unfolding the sordid tale to a stunned courtroom. Aside from the five women she'd murdered, Wood said, Graham had attempted to suffocate at least five others.

Graham's attorney, on rebuttal, tried to portray Wood as a jilted lover, who wanted to exact revenge against Wood with vindictive lies. The jury disagreed. After deliberating for seven hours, they convicted Graham on five counts of first-degree murder. She was sentenced to six terms of life imprisonment without possibility of parole. For her part in the crimes, Cathy Wood was sent to prison for a term of 20 to 40 years.

Teet Haerm

Catrine da Costa was a pretty 28-year-old, a former model fallen on hard times due to her heroin addiction and reduced to earning her living in the murky world of street prostitution in Stockholm, Sweden. On June 10, 1984, Catrine was working her normal beat along Malmskillnadsgatan, Stockholm's main red light strip, when she disappeared. Five weeks later, some of her mutilated remains turned up in a garbage bag near Solna, north of Stockholm. The location of the find seemed ironic. It was close to the Department of Forensic Medicine, where police autopsies were performed. Another three weeks passed before more human remains were discovered, less than a mile away. The head and some of the internal organs were missing. They'd never be found.

Prostitute murders are not that unusual, even in a relatively low-crime country like Sweden. Yet the unique mutilations inflicted on the corpse made this murder stand out. The police, therefore, got their best pathologist on the case.

Dr. Teet Haerm was just 31 years old but already a rising star in his profession. He'd been published in a number of prestigious medical journals and been a keynote speaker at international forensic medicine conferences. He was considered an expert in the forensics of strangulation murders – all of this while overcoming personal tragedy in the suicide of his wife and having to raise his four-year-old daughter on his own.

Dr. Haerm performed his examination on July 19, 1984, and concluded that the killer of Catrine de Costa was a man who was skilled at butchering animals. That sent the police scurrying to question every butcher they could track down, including one who had served time for killing and mutilating a prostitute. However, the man had an unbreakable alibi and that line of enquiry soon went cold.

A week later, the police again called on Dr. Haerm, when the strangled and mutilated corpse of 26-year-old prostitute Annika Mors was found in a public park. This time, Haerm changed his opinion of the perpetrator. Although he was confident that the same killer was responsible, Haerm now declared: "It is obvious that this man has a scalpel and knows how to use it. You don't find that kind of cutting edge on an ordinary knife. He knows precisely where all the internal organs are. Which makes it easy for him to remove the heart, the liver, the kidneys or the womb."

On August 1, another body turned up. She was Kristine Cravache, 27, a prostitute found naked and strangled in Stockholm's red light district. Over the weeks that followed, five more women – Lena Grans, Cats Falk, Lena Bofors, Lena Manson and Lota Svenson –

went missing. Not all of them were prostitutes, but the police were certain that all had fallen prey to the Stockholm serial killer.

One of these women, Lena Bofors, had in fact contacted the police and told them that she could identify the murderer. She'd also hinted that two men might be involved. A meeting was arranged but before it could take place, Bofors disappeared.

With public outrage growing and no real leads to go on, the police descended on the red light district and began questioning prostitutes. Over 600 streetwalkers were interviewed and a common thread soon began to emerge. Many of the women described a boyish, well-dressed man who drove a white, Volkswagen Rabbit. One witness said that this man had once beaten her up and she'd written down his license plate number, intending to report him. She'd later decided against involving the police, but she still had the number. Investigators ran it through the system and were stunned at the result. It belonged to Dr. Teet Haerm.

Haerm was brought in for questioning, while the police carried out a search of his home. There they found something extremely disturbing - a picture of his dead wife, blue in the face, a rope knotted around her neck. It appeared that Ann Catherine Haerm might not have committed suicide after all.

But the picture didn't amount to evidence of murder and, with nothing to link Haerm to the mutilation-slayings, he was released. Shortly after, he was fired from his job. In the meanwhile, the police were trying to find additional evidence that would either tie Haerm to the Stockholm murders or clear him as a suspect.

In March 1985, the bodies of missing prostitutes Lena Grans and Cats Falk were found together, in a car submerged at Hammarby dock. The mutilations inflicted on their bodies were similar to those in the earlier cases. On January 7, 1986, Tazunga Toyonaga, a Japanese student, was found dead in Copenhagen, Denmark. Although geographically removed from the other victims, the mutilations to the body suggested the same killer.

Yet despite these discoveries, the police were no closer to making an arrest. If Haerm was the serial killer they sought, he'd done a good job of covering his tracks. The investigators were beginning to despair that the case would never be solved when, out of nowhere, they caught a break.

In October 1987, a kindergarten teacher at a Stockholm school reported to police that she believed one of her young pupils was being sexually abused. The girl turned out to be the daughter of Dr. Allgren Thomas, a GP at a local hospital. Thomas initially denied the charges, but under sustained questioning, he eventually broke down and admitted to abusing his daughter. Then he stunned investigators by confessing that he was involved in the murders of the seven Stockholm serial killer victims. He hadn't killed the women himself, he said, but he'd been present when Dr. Teet Haerm had committed the murders.

According to Thomas, he and Haerm would troll the streets looking for a girl working alone. They'd offer her money to attend a sex party at Haerm's home, but as soon as the woman entered the house, they'd overpower her and Haerm would strangle her. They'd then take turns at committing necrophilia on the corpse. Later, they'd carry the body into the garage and dismember it. But not before Haerm had carved some flesh from the victim, cooked and eaten it. It was all part of a Druid ritual to assimilate the soul of the deceased, Thomas said.

Teet Haerm was arrested on October 28, 1987, and charged with the murders of the seven Stockholm victims, plus the Japanese student killed in Copenhagen. He was also indicted for the murder of his wife.

The trial commenced a year later and was a sensation in Sweden, with the public split on whether Haerm was guilty or not. In a highly controversial move, Haerm's five-year-old daughter emerged as a prosecution witness. The child had apparently witnessed the decapitation and dissection of Catrine da Costa and demonstrated to the court what had happened by removing the head of a doll. "They threw the head away, and then the lady was chopped up," the little girl said.

The defense immediately seized on the fact that the girl would only have been 18-months-old at the time of the murder and could not possibly have understood, let alone recalled, such a traumatic event. Nonetheless, the jury was prepared to buy it. On September 16, 1988, they returned a guilty verdict to the Stockholm District Court.

However, the story had one more twist to offer. Before the judge could formally confirm the verdict, a number of jurors gave interviews to the press, resulting in the High Court overturning the conviction. A subsequent retrial saw both of the defendants acquitted.

Teet Haerm and Allgren Thomas were set free. They remain at liberty, but with their reputations and livelihoods destroyed.

Beverley Allitt

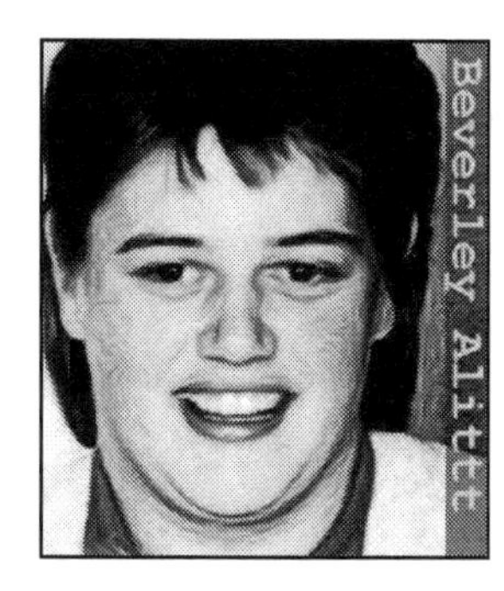

Medical practitioners, whether doctors or nurses, are placed in a unique position of trust. Quite literally, we trust them with our lives. But what if one of these individuals, for whatever reason, decides to do harm to those in their care? When this happens, the results can be catastrophic, as more than 200 victims of Dr. Harold Shipman found out to their cost. Beverley Allitt did not murder nearly as many as Shipman, but in many ways her crimes are even more shocking. This is because Allitt targeted the most vulnerable victims of all. She killed babies.

How Allitt ever came to be a nurse is a stern indictment on the systems in place to filter out individuals like her. One of four children, she exhibited some worrying signs early on. As a child, she enjoyed wearing bandages and casts and drawing awareness to her numerous ailments as a way of getting attention. And as she grew into an overweight adolescent, the behavior became even more pronounced. She took to spending considerable time at hospitals for a whole series of afflictions - gall bladder and urinary infections, headaches, vomiting, blurred vision, appendicitis, back trouble, and ulcers, to name just a few. She even, at one stage, convinced a doctor to remove a perfectly healthy appendix. Then, once the operation was completed, she took to picking at the surgical scar, preventing it from healing. She also indulged in other forms of self-harm, injuring herself with a hammer and with shards of glass. When one doctor cottoned on to her game, she simply moved on to another and began the charade all over again.

There is, of course, a name for this condition. It's called Munchausen's Syndrome, but by the time Allitt signed up to train as a nurse, she had not yet been diagnosed with it.

Allitt was a poor trainee, with an exceptionally high number of sick days and dire results in both written and practical examinations. She also displayed some odd behavior at the nursing home where she trained. She was suspected, for example, of smearing feces on a wall, and putting it into a refrigerator for others to find. Her boyfriend at the time also describes troubling signs. He says she was aggressive, manipulative and deceptive. On several occasions she claimed (falsely) to be pregnant. She also insisted that she'd been raped.

Yet, despite all of these warning signs, despite her failure to complete her nursing examinations, Allitt gained a temporary six-month placement at Grantham and Kesteven Hospital in Lincolnshire. The hospital was chronically understaffed and the ward Allitt was assigned to – Children's Ward 4 – had only two trained nurses on the day shift and one for nights. This is perhaps why Allitt was able to commit four murders, and attempt nine more.

The first victim was seven-month-old Liam Taylor, admitted to Ward 4 with a chest infection on February 21, 1991. Allitt went out of her way to meet Liam's parents and assure them that he would get the best possible care. She urged them to go home and get some rest. When the Taylors returned, Allitt told them that Liam had taken a turn for the worse and had required emergency care. However, she assured the concerned parents, he had come through it and was on the mend. She even volunteered for extra night duty so that she could be on hand if he needed her. The Taylors thanked her and said that they would spend the night at the hospital as well.

Just before midnight, while Allitt was alone with Liam, his condition suddenly worsened dramatically. He turned deathly pale and red blotches appeared on his skin and he began to have trouble breathing. Allitt shouted for an emergency resuscitation team, but their efforts were in vain. The little boy went into cardiac arrest, which resulted in irreversible brain damage. He was being kept alive only by life support machines and, on medical advice, his distraught parents made the heart-wrenching decision to turn off the support systems. Liam's cause of death was recorded as heart failure.

Yet the other nurses on the ward were confused. Why hadn't the alarm sounded when Liam had first stopped breathing? Only one person knew the answer, and Allitt was never questioned about the incident.

On March 5, 1991, just two weeks after Liam's death, Timothy Hardwick was admitted to Ward 4. The 11-year-old boy had cerebral palsy, and had suffered an epileptic fit. Allitt immediately took over his care, making a great show of her concern for the patient. However, she'd only been alone with Timothy for a few minutes when she raced out of the ward shouting that he'd gone into cardiac arrest. By the time the emergency resuscitation team arrived, Timothy had stopped breathing and was turning blue. Despite their desperate efforts, the team was unable to revive him. Epilepsy was officially recorded as the cause of death.

Five days later, one-year-old Kayley Desmond, who had been admitted to Ward 4 on March 3, went into cardiac arrest after being attended by Allitt. The little girl had been brought in with a chest infection but had appeared to be recovering well. Fortunately, the resuscitation team was able to revive her and she was transferred to another hospital in Nottingham, where she made a full recovery. The attending physicians at Nottingham did, however, discover an odd puncture mark under her armpit. This was attributed to an accidental injection and no further action was taken.

Perhaps frustrated by her latest victim's escape, Allitt stepped up her activities, attacking three children over the next four days.

Five-month-old Paul Crampton had been placed in Ward 4 on March 20, as a result of a minor bronchial infection. On the day Paul was due to be discharged, Allitt was again attending him alone, when she called out that he was suffering from insulin shock. The emergency team rushed to the scene and doctors fought desperately to save Paul's life. Three times he slipped into a near-coma and three times they were able to revive him. Yet the doctors were flummoxed as to why his blood sugar kept dropping.

Eventually, they were able to stabilize the boy and he was sent by ambulance to a hospital in Nottingham. Allitt rode with him, and on arrival, his insulin levels were again found to be elevated. Happily, little Paul survived the attentions of the Angel of Death, but it was only by a whisker.

The following day, five-year-old Bradley Gibson, suffering from pneumonia, went into cardiac arrest but was saved by the emergency resuscitation team. Blood tests showed perplexingly high levels of insulin but the boy's condition was stabilized and he appeared to be recovering. Then, after a late night visit from Allitt, he suffered another heart attack. Bradley was transported to Nottingham, where he made a full recovery.

Amazingly, given the alarming increase in crisis situations since Allitt's arrival, no one seems to have asked any questions. She was left to continue her dirty work unchecked.

On March 22, Allitt again raised the alarm after two-year-old Yik Hung Chan turned blue and appeared to have difficulty breathing. The boy was resuscitated with oxygen but later suffered a relapse after being left alone with Allitt. He was then transferred to Nottingham, where he recovered fully. His symptoms were attributed to a fractured skull he'd suffered as the result of a fall.

Allitt next turned her attention to two-month-old twins, Katie and Becky Phillips. The girls had been born prematurely, but after an extended stay in the hospital had been sent home in good health. Then Becky suffered a bout of gastroenteritis and was brought to Ward 4 on April 1, 1991. Two days later, Allitt raised an alarm, claiming that Becky appeared hypoglycemic and was cold to the touch. However, the response team found nothing wrong with her and she was discharged that evening.

During the night, Becky suffered convulsions and a doctor was summoned, who diagnosed colic. Her parents kept her in their bed for observation, but she died during the night. An autopsy was unable to find a clear cause of death.

As a precautionary measure, Becky's surviving twin, Katie, was admitted to Ward 4, where Allitt was again in attendance. It wasn't long before a resuscitation team was rushing to the ward to revive Katie. Although their efforts were successful, Katie suffered a similar attack two days later. She was rushed to Nottingham, but on arrival, it was found that she'd suffered irreversible brain damage as a result of oxygen deprivation.

Yet Katie survived and her grateful mother, still devastated by the loss of Becky, asked Allitt to be Katie's godmother. Allitt coyly accepted, even though she was responsible for inflicting paralysis, cerebral palsy, and sight and hearing damage on the baby.

Allitt must have thought by now that she was invincible, that she could continue attacking children with impunity. Certainly, no one at Grantham was raising any questions about the sudden spate of deadly incidents in Ward 4. Unbeknownst to Allitt, suspicions were being raised at the Nottingham hospital that many of the young victims had been sent to. Still, it would take four more attacks, and another death, before Allitt was finally found out.

Fifteen-month-old Claire Peck was brought into Grantham on April 22, 1991. Claire was an asthmatic who required a breathing tube. The child had been in Allitt's care for only a few minutes when the emergency team had to be called in for the first time. They managed to revive her, but a short while later Clare suffered a second heart attack and died.

In the wake of Claire's death, Dr. Nelson Porter, a consultant at Grantham, initiated an inquiry. The high number of cardiac arrests on Ward 4, over the previous two months, alarmed him. Yet even now, Allitt seems to have escaped suspicion. The hospital believed that an airborne virus might be to blame, although tests turned up negative. Then the autopsy results from baby Claire revealed an inordinately high level of potassium in the blood, caused by the presence of Lignocaine. This drug is commonly used during cardiac arrest but should never be given to a baby. Belatedly, the hospital called the police.

Superintendant Stuart Clifton, the officer assigned to the investigation, looked at the other suspicious incidents over the previous two months and immediately suspected foul play. His suspicions were firmed up when it was revealed that all of the victims had unusually high doses of insulin or potassium in their blood streams. Further investigation revealed that the key to the insulin refrigerator had been reported missing – by Beverley Allitt. And a check on daily nursing logs turned up another curious detail. Several pages corresponding to the near-fatal attack on Paul Crampton were missing.

As the police checked and rechecked records, interviewed staff and spoke to parents of the victims, a common denominator began to emerge. In 25 separate suspicious incidents, involving 13 victims, and resulting in four deaths, the only constant was Beverley Allitt.

Within three weeks of the police being notified, Allitt was arrested. She remained calm under interrogation and steadfastly maintained her innocence. However, a search of her home revealed the missing pages from the nursing log, throwing such assertions into question. Further investigation revealed a pattern of behavior congruent with a very serious personality disorder. Psychologists who examined Allitt believed that she exhibited symptoms of both Munchausen's Syndrome, and Munchausen's Syndrome by Proxy (MSbP). Munchausen's is characterized by attempting to gain attention through illness, while MSbP involves inflicting injury on others to gain attention for oneself. It is highly unusual for an individual to present with both conditions.

In November 1991, Allitt was formally charged with four counts of murder, eleven counts of attempted murder, and eleven counts of causing grievous bodily harm. She eventually went on trial at Nottingham Crown Court on February 15, 1993. In the intervening period, she had developed anorexia nervosa, and lost over 60 pounds in weight.

The evidence against Allitt was overwhelming. Prosecutors were able to show how she was present at every suspicious incident and how such incidents stopped immediately after she was removed from her post. They were able to show high readings of insulin and potassium in each of the victims, as well as unexplained needle puncture marks. Allitt was further accused of cutting off her victims' oxygen, either by smothering or by tampering with equipment. A psychologist explained Munchausen's syndrome and Munchausen's by Proxy syndrome and showed that Allitt demonstrated symptoms of both. Allitt provided ample proof of this herself. During a trial that lasted 2 months, she was in court only 16 days, being too "ill" to attend on the other days.

The trial eventually concluded on May 23, 1993, with a guilty verdict and a sentence of 13 life sentences, the harshest ever handed down to a female defendant in British history.

Allitt was incarcerated at Rampton Secure Hospital, a high-security facility in Nottingham that houses individuals detained under the Mental Health Act. But even here, she continued her attention seeking behavior, stabbing herself with paperclips, ingesting ground glass, and scalding herself with boiling water.

She subsequently admitted to three of the murders, as well as several of the assaults. It is extremely unlikely that she will ever be released.

Orville Lynn Majors

Nursing is a tough profession, which demands a lot of its practitioners. Those who take up the calling are faced daily with death and disease, long, physically demanding work hours, and patients who can often be difficult. Quite aside from their technical qualifications, nurses require an abundance of patience, a natural empathy, and a genuine desire to serve their fellow man. The vast majority, possess these qualities in abundance. Others, unfortunately, do not.

One has to wonder what it was exactly that attracted Orville Lynn Majors to the nursing profession. He seems to have been horribly unsuited to his chosen vocation, genuinely antagonistic towards the elderly patients under his care. One of the kinder epithets he applied to them was "wasters." He also complained to acquaintances that the patients took pleasure in making his life difficult and that he hated their whining. They all deserved to be gassed, he said, although few would have believed that he meant this literally.

Orville Lynn Majors was born on April 24, 1961, in Clinton, Indiana. Little is known about his early life and upbringing, but we do know that, as a teen, he cared for his ailing grandmother. Perhaps this is what sparked his interest in a nursing career because after finishing high school he enrolled at a training school in Nashville, Tennessee, emerging eventually with an LPN (Licensed Practical Nurse) qualification. Thereafter, he quickly found work at the 56-bed Vermillion County Hospital in his hometown.

Majors was, by all accounts, regarded as a compassionate and hard-working employee. But he must have found that nursing did not match up to his expectations because he quit soon after. Then, unable to find alternative employment, he reapplied at Vermillion and was accepted. Not long after that, administrators began to notice a rise in death rates at the hospital.

This was no gentle escalation either. In 1992, twenty-six patients had died at Vermillion. Two years later, that number had soared to 101, most of the deaths occurring in the 4-bed ICU. In the latter six months of 1994 alone, 67 people died. There were days when all four ICU patients expired.

Something clearly had to be done, and the hospital, therefore, brought in an expert to investigate. The consultant began by studying patient charts and nurses' time cards. Immediately, he picked up a pattern, something so glaringly obvious that it was a miracle no one had spotted it earlier. The majority of deaths at the hospital had a common denominator, ICU nurse, Orville Lynn Majors.

The escalation in the death rate at the hospital coincided almost exactly with the beginning of Majors' employment there. In the four prior years, no more than 31 patients had died in any single year. Then, over the 22 months that Majors worked at Vermillion, 147 died in the ICU, 121 of them while Majors was on duty. To put that into context, a death occurred every 23 hours when Majors was on duty. When he wasn't working, a death occurred every 551 hours. That means that patients were 43 times more likely to die on Majors' shift than on any other.

This was not, of course, proof of any wrongdoing. However, it had to be reported to the authorities and the subsequent investigation soon firmed up the consultant's suspicions. First, a quantity of potassium chloride was found in Majors' home and in his van. Then a round of exhumations uncovered symptoms consistent with an overdose of that particular drug, which would cause an abrupt rise in blood pressure before the patient's heart suddenly stopped. Perhaps most tellingly, the death rate at the hospital dropped dramatically after Majors was suspended from his job in the wake of the investigation.

Orville Lynn Majors went on trial for murder in October 1999. Although he was suspected of as many as 130 murders he was tried for only seven; Mary Ann Alderson, 69; Dorothea Hixon, 80; Cecil Smith, 74; Luella Hopkins, 89; Margaret Hornick, 79; Freddie Wilson, 56; and Derek Maxwell Sr., 64.

And the evidence in these seven cases was pretty damning, with a number of eyewitnesses coming forward to testify that they had seen Majors giving injections to patients. So blatant was the killer that he would even inject his victims in front of their loved ones.

One such instance was the case of Dorothea Hixon. Mrs. Hixon's daughter, Paula Holdaway, was visiting her mother when Majors walked in and said that he needed to give Mrs. Hixon an injection. He then brushed the octogenarian's hair aside, kissed her forehead, and said, "It's all right pumpkin, everything's going to be all right now." Within a minute of Majors injecting her, Mrs. Hixon's eyes rolled back and she died.

Despite this, and other evidence, the defense team sought to cast reasonable doubt on the accusations. They wanted to know, for example, why the police had focused their investigation solely on Majors when other doctors and nurses had equal access to the patients. It was a question that was never satisfactorily resolved during the six-week trial, but it was not one that deterred the jury from a guilty verdict on six of the charges. In the other case, that of Cecil Smith, Judge Ernest Yelton declared a mistrial.

In the end, it was Majors injudicious comments about his elderly patients that sealed his fate. He was sentenced to six terms of 60 years – a total of 360 years in prison – to be served consecutively. Theoretically, Majors will have to spend 180 years behind bars before he becomes eligible for parole.

The Lainz Angels of Death

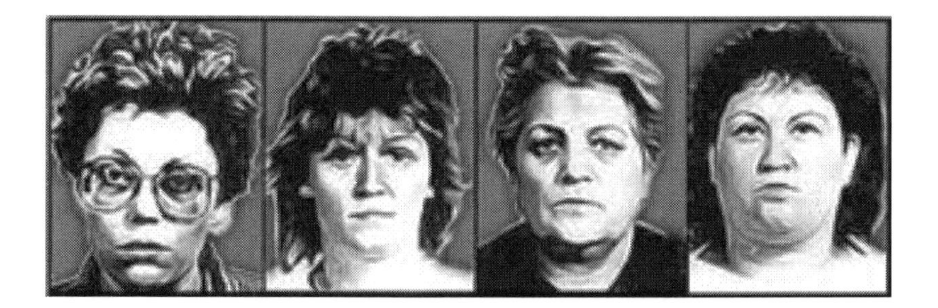

The Lainz General Hospital is one of the largest medical facilities in Vienna, Austria, a sprawling complex with a staff of some 2,000 medics and support personnel. Within Lainz General, Pavilion 5 is reserved for elderly patients, many of them in the latter stages of terminal illness. Unsurprisingly, the ward has a high mortality rate.

However, between the years 1983 and 1989, not all of the deaths in Pavilion 5 were from natural causes. A killer was at work among the elderly patients, claiming at least 42 lives, and possibly as many as 300.

It all began in the spring of '83 when a 77-year-old female patient approached a nurses' aide named Waltraud Wagner with an unusual request. She wanted Wagner to overdose her with an injection of morphine, thereby ending her suffering.

At first, Wagner was reluctant. She had, after all, entered the nursing profession to preserve life, not take it. But eventually the patient's desperate pleas won her over and she agreed to carry out the mercy killing. She duly delivered the lethal shot. To her surprise, she realized that the act of murder, of playing God, thrilled her. She could hardly wait for an opportunity to "terminate" another patient.

No one knows how many patients Wagner killed on her own before she decided to enlist others into her death scheme. What we do know is that over time, she recruited three accomplices, all of them nursing aides working the night shift in Pavilion 5.

Maria Gruber, 19, Irene Leidolf, 21, and Stephanija Mayer, a 43-year-old immigrant from Yugoslavia, all agreed to join in the deadly business. And their targets were no longer the terminally ill. Any patient who annoyed them was considered fair game and these annoyances didn't even have to be serious. Anyone who snored too much, or wet the bed, or refused to take medication, or buzzed the nurses' station too often or at inconvenient times, might be targeted.

Once a patient was marked for death, Wagner would announce to her followers, "This one gets a ticket to God." The victim would then receive a visit from the deadly foursome during the night.

At first, the Lainz "Angels" dispatched their victims with fatal doses of morphine or insulin. But those methods soon lost their novelty value and when lethal injection failed to deliver the requisite thrill, Wagner devised another method, one she called her "water cure." The patients' nose would be pinched, her head forced back and the tongue depressed. Water would then be poured down her throat, slowly drowning her, a particularly painful death. As it is common for elderly patients to die with fluid in their lungs, these deaths did not arouse suspicion.

The killers also took pains to restrain their murderous instincts. Wagner, as the de facto leader, made the calls as to who would die and chose her victims carefully. But typical of most serial killers she became more and more confident as each new death went undiscovered. Then, after Mayer rounded out the group in 1987, the murder rate accelerated. By 1988, so many deaths were occurring in Pavilion 5 that it had acquired the nickname, "Pavilion of death." There were rumors of a killer working the ward but if hospital administrators got to hear of it, they took no action. As so often happens in these cases, it would take an act of stunning recklessness by the perpetrators to finally bring their heinous deeds to light.

The "Death Angels" were in the habit of adjourning to a local tavern for a few drinks after their shift. The topic of conversation on these occasions most often turned to the murders they'd committed. February 23, 1989, was no different. The nurses sat in their usual spot, whispering and giggling together as they discussed the murder of an elderly patient named Julia Drapal. Mrs. Drapal had been given the water cure for refusing medication and for calling Waltraud Wagner a "common slut." The foursome appeared particularly amused by the expression on the old woman's face just before she died.

Unfortunately for the "Angels," a doctor was seated at the next table and overheard snatches of their conversation. Horrified by what he'd heard, he went to the police and an undercover investigation was launched. Six weeks later, on April 7, all four suspects found themselves under arrest, charged with multiple counts of murder.

Once in custody, the four women appeared to have no problem at all admitting to their crimes. Wagner, in particular, seemed to relish her role, claiming 39 murders on her own and ten more with various accomplices. "I killed those who got on my nerves," she proclaimed proudly. "Dispatched them directly to a free bed with the good Lord."

However, she was singing a different tune when she heard that the other "Angels" had placed most of the blame on her. Then she changed her story, now claiming that she'd only killed ten patients and that those had been mercy killings, carried out after the victims had begged her to end their suffering. It made no difference to prosecutors. In March 1991, Wagner and her accomplices went on trial, charged with the most brutal murder spree in Austria's peacetime history.

The prosecution initially sought to prove 42 counts of murder, but, in the end, had to be satisfied with 15 convictions against Wagner and five against Leidolf. Both were sentenced to life in prison. Stephanija Mayer and Maria Gruber, meanwhile, were convicted on various charges of manslaughter and attempted murder. They each drew terms of 15 years in prison.

Yet the heartless killers would serve only a portion of those sentences. Mayer and Gruber were released in 2003, having spent 13 years behind bars. Five years later, in 2008, Leidolf and Wagner walked free, having served just 18 years of their life sentences. The early releases sparked widespread outrage in Austria and the "Lainz Angels of Death," perhaps wisely, disappeared from public life.

Charles Cullen

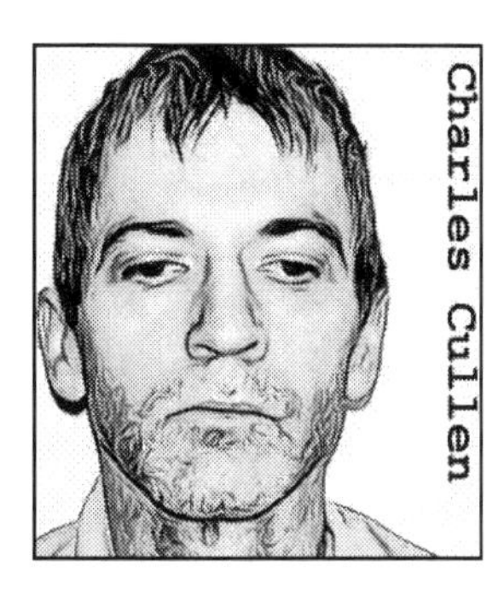

When administrators at Somerset Medical Center in Somerville, New Jersey installed a state-of-the-art computerized care system, they could never have imagined that it would lead to the apprehension of America's most deadly medical serial killer.

The system, called Cerner, allowed nurses to check a patient's medical history at a computer terminal. It also managed the dispensing of drugs, opening a drawer that allowed medical staff to withdraw meds as required.

On the night shift of June 15, 2003, someone ordered digoxin (a heart medication) for a patient, then promptly canceled the order. It seemed a genuine mistake, the patient did not have a heart problem and the medication had not been prescribed for them. However, the drug itself disappeared from stock.

And there was other suspicious activity on Cerner that night.

Someone accessed the records of 44-year-old cancer patient, Jin Kyung Han. Innocuous in itself, except that the patient went into cardiac arrest the next morning and doctors were stunned to find high levels of digoxin in her system. Han was given an antidote and stabilized. But who had given her digoxin in the first place?

A couple of weeks later, 68-year-old Reverend Florian Gall, a Roman Catholic priest, suffered a heart attack at the same hospital. Again, high levels of digoxin were found, although in Gall's case this was to be expected – he was a heart patient. The levels of the drug, though, seemed suspiciously high - too high to have been administered accidentally.

Hospital administrators launched an internal investigation. And with their sophisticated computer system, they should have noticed something awry. Prior to both patients' cardiac arrests, a nurse by the name of Charles Cullen had accessed the system to order digoxin. He'd soon canceled both orders, but the drugs themselves were missing. If administrators picked this up, they chose to ignore it.

But Steven Marcus, executive director at the New Jersey Poison Information System, had also detected a troubling trend, a cluster of four patient deaths that didn't look right. When he flagged these to SMC and suggested they may have an "angel of death" on their staff, they reacted angrily, reporting Marcus to State medical administrators. Yet despite their protests, SMC must have had their own suspicions. When two more patients suffered overdoses of digoxin on October 31, Charles Cullen was fired.

Meanwhile, Somerset County Prosecutor Wayne Forrest had started his own investigation into Cullen. He began by looking into Cullen's work history and found that he'd been employed at an alarmingly high number of healthcare organizations, and been fired from many of them. He also discovered that Cullen had been investigated at other hospitals, on suspicion of having harmed patients.

Even so, Cullen remained at large. It wasn't until December 12, 2003, that he was eventually arrested and charged with the murder of Reverend Florian Gall and the attempted murder of Jin Kyung Han. In both cases, it was suspected that Cullen had administered potentially lethal doses of digoxin, which he had obtained by manipulating the hospital's computer system. Cullen didn't seem to realize that canceling an order doesn't remove it from the system. He'd left a trail.

Cullen didn't resist his arrest. In fact, he made it clear that he had no intention of fighting the charges against him. He also stunned investigators by revealing that these incidents were only the tip of the iceberg. He'd been killing for 16 years, he said, and during that time he'd deliberately overdosed between 30 and 40 patients in ten different hospitals. That would make him the most deadly healthcare serial killer in US history.

Cullen fully expected that he'd get the death penalty and seemed resigned to that fate, pleading guilty at his arraignment and rescinding his request for a court appointed attorney. However, a week later, he changed his mind and agreed to meet with public defender, Johnnie Mask.

After consulting with Cullen, Mask got to work trying to keep his client off death row. He approached Pennsylvania and New Jersey prosecutors to propose a deal. Cullen would clear up cases in exchange for them waiving the death penalty. But both states had to agree to the deal, or it was off the table.

By now, the case was national news and media channels were rushing to find out more about the man who might turn out to be America's most prolific serial killer. Their investigations would reveal a depressed and deeply disturbed individual, who should never have been allowed to work in a profession where dispensing death is as easy as preserving life.

Charles Cullen was born in West Orange, New Jersey, the youngest of eight children in a strict Roman Catholic family. His father was 58 years old at the time of Charles' birth and died when the boy was just seven months old. His mother was killed in an automobile accident when Charles was in high school.

Devastated by his mother's death, Cullen dropped out of school and enlisted in the Navy. He was assigned to the submarine corps and did well, rising to the rank of petty officer third class. But he was also showing signs of mental instability. He once completed a shift dressed in a surgical gown, surgical mask and latex gloves stolen from the ship's medical cabinet. Deemed unfit for duty aboard a sub, he was transferred to the supply ship USS Canopus. Over the next few years, he tried several times to commit suicide, leading to a medical discharge from the Navy on March 30, 1984.

After leaving the military, Cullen enrolled at the Mountainside

Hospital School of Nursing. He also got married during this time, although the marriage would later break down. By 1988, he had graduated from Mountainside. Nursing diploma in hand, he took up a position at the burn unit of the St. Barnabas Medical Center.

When, exactly, Cullen committed his first murder is uncertain. Cullen himself is sketchy on the details, but investigators believe it may have been in June 1988. Judge John W. Yengo Sr. had been admitted following an allergic reaction to a blood-thinning medication. He died after Cullen injected a drug into his IV unit. Cullen admitted to killing several other patients while at St. Barnabas. He later quit in the wake of allegations that he had deliberately contaminated IV bags with insulin.

Cullen's next job was at Warren Hospital in Phillipsburg, New Jersey in February 1992. There, he murdered three elderly women with overdoses of digoxin. One of his victims was Helen Dean, a 91-year-old cancer sufferer. During one visit, Mrs. Dean complained to her son that Cullen had jabbed her with a needle while she slept. Larry Dean raised the issue with nursing staff, but no one seemed to take his complaint seriously.

The following day, Mrs. Dean suffered a fatal heart attack. Her son demanded action, but an investigation found no evidence that any crime had been committed. Larry Dean continued to believe that his mother had been murdered, but he passed away himself before seeing justice done. His belief would be vindicated after Charles Cullen eventually confessed to the crime.

Cullen's wife divorced him in January 1993, citing negligence and domestic violence. Cullen got joint custody of his two daughters, but the divorce devastated him. In March 1993, he broke into the home of a co-worker and received a year's probation. Cullen then started following the woman around and calling her on the phone until she obtained a restraining order against him. He made three more suicide attempts during 1993 and spent two separate spells in psychiatric facilities before the year was out, receiving treatment for depression.

In December 1993, Cullen resigned from Warren Hospital and moved to the Hunterdon Medical Center in Flemington, New Jersey. He would spend three years here and claims that he committed no murders during this time. Given his previous proficiency, this seems unlikely, but hospital records for the period had been destroyed by the time of Cullen's arrest, making it impossible to check.

Cullen's next job was at Morristown Memorial Hospital in Morristown, New Jersey. He was dismissed for poor work performance in August 1997 and thereafter remained unemployed for six months. The loss of his job seems to have affected him badly and his behavior became increasingly bizarre during this period. Neighbors reported him making faces at them, talking to himself and standing in the middle of the street, in the dead of night, shouting at the sky.

Yet, despite these worrying signs, Cullen had another nursing job in February 1998, this time at Liberty Nursing Center in Allentown, Pennsylvania. While Cullen was employed here, another nurse would be fired for causing the death of a patient named Francis Henry, who Cullen would later admit to killing with an overdose of insulin. Cullen lasted just seven months at Liberty, before he was dismissed for trying to administer an unscheduled injection to a patient.

But the loss of yet another job had done nothing to curb Charles Cullen's murderous instincts. While working at Easton Hospital in Easton, Pennsylvania, in December 1998, Cullen murdered 78-year-old Ottomar Schramm. Northampton County coroner Zachary Lysek's report showed lethal levels of digoxin in the patient's bloodstream, and Lysek raised concerns that there might be an "angel of death" working at Easton. But despite an internal investigation, nothing pointed conclusively to Cullen.

And still the killing continued. Cullen's next port of call was Lehigh Valley Hospital in Allentown, Pennsylvania. Here, he murdered at least one patient before moving on to St. Luke's Hospital in Bethlehem, Pennsylvania, in April 1999.

Cullen enjoyed a longer tenure here, staying for three years during which time he killed another five patients. His employment was eventually terminated in June 2002, after a co-worker discovered vials of unused drugs hidden in a disposal bin. These were traced to Cullen and he was fired after an internal investigation.

By then, seven of Cullen's nursing colleagues at St. Luke's had already met with the Lehigh County district attorney to raise their suspicions about the high number of patients that were dying under Cullen's care. An investigation was launched, but it led nowhere and was eventually dropped. Later it would emerge that hospital administrators had been less than forthcoming with investigators.

And so, in September 2002, Charles Cullen moved on to what would be his last job, at Somerset Medical Center in New Jersey. Eight patients would die by his hand here before his dismissal and subsequent arrest.

Under interrogation, Cullen admitted that he had intended the deaths of the patients he had killed. But, in typical serial killer fashion, he shifted the blame for the crimes to others. He boasted about how easy it was to go from one institution to another, moving on as soon as suspicions were aroused. He even claimed that his superiors knew what was going on, but simply looked the other way.

In April 2004, Cullen entered a guilty plea to 13 counts of first-degree murder in a New Jersey court. A month later, he pled guilty to killing three more patients in New Jersey. In November 2004, he accepted responsibility for six murders in Pennsylvania.

Charles Cullen is currently serving his life sentence at New Jersey State Prison in Trenton, New Jersey. He is ineligible for parole for 397 years.

But the murders committed by Cullen had implications that went way beyond this case. In the wake of his conviction, a plethora of legislation was enacted to avoid the possibility of another medical serial killer like Cullen, or his contemporary, Donald Harvey.

The reason that Cullen was able to move from facility to facility, murdering at will, can be directly attributed to the lax reporting requirements of the era. Health care facilities were only required to report suspicious deaths in the most blatant of negligence cases, and the penalties for failing to report were minor. In addition, employers were reluctant to investigate negligence issues, as it exposed them to potential lawsuits. And even if an inquiry were launched, legislation prevented investigators from delving into an employee's previous work record.

The Cullen case changed that. In its wake, most states introduced new laws that strengthened disclosure requirements for health care facilities, and mandated background criminal checks for all health care employees. It was a step in the right direction, but one that offered scant consolation to those who had lost friends and relatives to the medical monster that was Charles Cullen.

Arnfinn Nesset

He made the unlikeliest of serial killers, a balding, bespectacled and mild-mannered nursing home administrator, who was well liked by his patients and valued by his employers. And yet, Arnfinn Nesset enters the record book as the deadliest Scandinavian serial killer of all time. Suspected of 138 murders, he was eventually convicted of 22.

Born in Trondelag, Norway in 1936, Nesset never knew his father and was raised solely by his mother. This sort of domestic situation has been noted as a commonality in serial killer cases, but Nesset appeared to be a happy and balanced, if somewhat shy, child. After completing school, he qualified as a registered nurse, excelling at that profession and working his way through the ranks.

By the time he was appointed as administrator of the Orkdale Valley Nursing Home in 1977, Nesset had enjoyed a 20-year nursing career during which he'd built up an exemplary record. Orkdale is a geriatric care facility, where deaths are frequent and expected. Still, there appeared to be a spike in the mortality rate shortly after Nesset took up his post. This higher rate continued over the next three years and was eventually accepted by hospital staff as the norm. Nobody suspected that a killer might be at work until 1981 when a renewed spate of baffling deaths raised concern.

At around the same time, an employee at the clinic noticed that administrator Nesset had recently placed an unusually large order for Curacit, a muscle relaxant that is derived from curare, the poison used by indigenous South American tribes on the tips of their hunting arrows. Uncertain what to do with the information, the staff member passed it on to a local journalist, who went to the police.

Nesset, 46 years old at the time, was brought in for questioning. He readily admitted to ordering the Curacit, but insisted that there was a perfectly innocent reason behind it. A pack of feral dogs had been hanging around the clinic, rummaging through garbage and generally causing a nuisance. According to Nesset, he'd bought the drug to poison them.

It seemed a reasonable explanation. But with the police apparently prepared to accept his version of events, Nesset suddenly changed tack. “I killed them,” he told stunned investigators. “I've killed so many over the years that I'm unable to remember them all.”

He then began a rambling confession, in which he claimed that he'd started killing soon after beginning his nursing career in 1962. He'd murdered patients in three other institutions, he said, always using the same method, curare poisoning.

With officers now scrambling to verify the details of Nesset's earlier murders, Nesset was sent for psychiatric evaluation and found fit to stand trial. Meanwhile, the police turned up 68 suspicious deaths at the institutions where he'd previously been employed. They soon dismissed the possibility of charging Nesset for any of those crimes. Curare breaks down quickly in the human body and the presence of the poison becomes increasingly difficult to trace over time. When the charge sheet was eventually drawn up it included the 27 murders Nesset had confessed to, all of them committed at Orkdale Valley. He was also charged with forgery and embezzlement, relating to money misappropriated from his victims.

Nessett went on trial in October 1982, but the day before court proceedings were due to start, he threw prosecutors a curveball by suddenly retracting his confessions. That left the prosecution having to prove murder, no easy task despite the presence of Curacit in the victims' bodies and Nesset's signature on the purchase orders. Five months and 128 witnesses later, prosecutors eventually had their desired outcome. Arnfinn Nesset was found guilty on 22 counts of willful murder.

Yet one crucial question was never satisfactorily answered at the trial. Why had he done it? Why had this apparently dedicated medical professional so wantonly murdered the patients under his care?

Nesset himself provided a series of conflicting motives. First he said that the murders were mercy killings, then he blamed his schizophrenia, then he said that he was "making room" for new patients at the crowded clinic. Finally, he admitted that he had killed for the morbid pleasure it gave him. Arnfinn Nesset was just a common murderer after all.

Not that any of this affected the decision of the court. Nesset was sentenced to 21 years in prison, the harshest penalty possible under Norwegian law. He would serve just 12 of those years before his release in 2004.

After gaining his freedom, Nesset promptly disappeared. He is believed to be living under an assumed name, somewhere in Norway.

Kristen Gilbert

Kristen Gilbert was born Kristen Strickland on November 13, 1967. When she was six months old, her family relocated to Fall River, Massachusetts, where Kristen would later be enrolled in kindergarten. She was a happy, lively child, although her demeanor changed somewhat after the birth of her younger sister. Kristen, seven years old at the time, seemed to resent the attention given to her sibling. She responded by inventing ailments and illnesses and by telling tall tales. One of her favorites was that she was related to Lizzie Borden, the infamous axe murderess who had lived in Fall River.

This almost obsessive need for attention only seemed to deepen as Kristen grew older. Although popular with boys, she seldom maintained a relationship for very long, due to her neurotic, overly possessive behavior. When a relationship inevitably broke down, she'd become abusive. More than one former boyfriend found his home or car vandalized. Some even reported threats of physical violence.

These negative traits notwithstanding, Kristen was an intelligent girl who graduated high school at age sixteen and thereafter enrolled on a nursing course at Greenfield Community College. In 1988, she gained certification as a registered nurse. Later that year, she married Glenn Gilbert and in 1989, she gained a position on the staff of the Veterans Hospital at Northampton, Massachusetts. An avid reader on medical matters, Kristen was an excellent and knowledgeable nurse. She was also pretty and photogenic, leading to her being featured on the cover of "VA Practitioner" magazine in April 1990.

Yet despite this stellar beginning to her nursing career, not all was well in the life of Kristen Gilbert. There were problems in her marriage harking right back to the honeymoon when she'd threatened her husband with a knife during an argument. Glen Gilbert had quickly learned that his wife was far from stable. She veered between elation and depression, threatened suicide on numerous occasions, and spent recklessly. She was also somewhat of a hypochondriac, a condition that seemed to intensify after the birth of her son in 1990.

And things at work were hardly much better. 1990 saw the beginning of a worrying pattern of patient deaths while Gilbert was on duty. No one suspected anything untoward, but the other nurses began to refer jokingly to Gilbert as the "Angel of Death."

Not everyone saw the humor in the situation, though. One alert clerical worker noticed that the death rate on the ward was three times higher when Gilbert was on duty. She reported her concerns to her superiors but was told not to make unfounded aspersions.

In November 1993, Kristen gave birth to a second son. By then, her marriage to Glen Gilbert was already in deep trouble and she was telling her work colleagues that she was thinking about a divorce. She had, in any case, cast her eye elsewhere, to a handsome hospital security guard named James Perrault. She began making a concerted effort to lose weight and started flirting openly with Perrault. It wasn't long before they were sneaking off to the parking lot to have sex in his car.

Shortly after Kristen began her affair with James Perrault, her husband Glen became seriously ill. He was taken to hospital where tests found extremely low potassium levels, a condition almost unheard of in a man of his age. It would later be speculated that Kristen had been feeding him drugs to suppress the mineral and thus elevate his blood pressure to dangerously high levels. A short while after Glen was hospitalized, the couple split, with Kristen moving into her own apartment, leaving the children in Glen's care.

Meanwhile, at the VA hospital, Kristen Gilbert's patients continued to die. On August 21, 1995, Gilbert was seen entering a ward holding a syringe. A short while later, Korean War veteran Stanley Jagodowski began shouting for a nurse, complaining that his arm hurt. Within minutes, he went into cardiac arrest. Despite the best efforts of medics, he died later that day. Over the months that followed, several other patients died in startlingly similar circumstances, all of them while Kristen Gilbert was on duty.

And yet, amazingly, hospital administrators failed to see anything unusual. It was only after three of Gilbert's colleagues raised concerns about the number of cardiac arrest deaths on the ward, that management agreed to take action. A subsequent enquiry noted that vials of epinephrine, a drug that mimics the effects of adrenaline, were missing. It was then that hospital managers called in the police.

The enquiry was far-reaching and included the exhumation of four patients, all of who were found to have high levels of epinephrine in their bodies. After supplies of the drug were found stashed at Gilbert's house, she was placed under arrest and charged with killing three patients - Henry Hudon, 35, Kenneth Cutting, 41, and Edward Skwira, 69 - and attempting to kill two more. A forth murder, that of Stanley Jagodowski, was later added to the rap sheet. Evidence suggested that Gilbert had injected her victims with epinephrine, causing their hearts to race out of control and eventually fail.

Why exactly Gilbert murdered her patients is unclear, although psychiatrists suggested that she was suffering from Munchausen by Proxy syndrome and wanted to draw attention to herself and her ability to deal with emergency situations. Specifically, they believe that she was trying to impress her lover, James Perrault. VA hospital rules mandate that hospital police must be present at any medical emergency, so Perrault was often in attendance.

And there were many emergency situations when Kristen Gilbert was on duty. Most of the patients survived, but of the 63 that didn't, 37 died under Kristen Gilbert's care. And that number may be only the tip of the iceberg. Investigators believe that Gilbert may have been responsible for as many as 80 deaths.

Kristen Gilbert was eventually convicted in federal court on March 14, 2001. Although Massachusetts does not have capital punishment, Gilbert was eligible for the death penalty, as her crimes had been committed on federal property.

However, a sentence of death requires a unanimous verdict on the part of the jury and as that was not achieved, the judgment defaulted automatically to life in prison without the possibility of parole. An additional 20 years was added for the attempted murder convictions.

Kristen Gilbert is currently incarcerated at a federal prison in Texas.

Harold Shipman

Kathleen Grundy was a vivacious widow with energy to burn and a great love of life. The wealthy 81-year-old had once served as the mayor of Hyde, Lancashire. She was a loved and respected member of the community, noted for her charity work. One of Kathleen's causes was the Age Concern Club, where she helped serve meals to elderly pensioners. She was passionate about this work and known for her punctuality and reliability. So when she didn't show up on June 24, 1998, her friends were immediately concerned. A few of them set off for Kathleen's home, where they found her lying on the sofa, fully dressed. When they'd last seen her, she'd been her usual chirpy self. Now, she was dead.

Kathleen Grundy had been a patient of Dr. Harold Shipman, who had, in fact, visited her just a few hours before her death. Mrs. Grundy's friends placed a call to Dr. Shipman and he arrived soon after and pronounced her dead.

A short while later, Mrs. Grundy's daughter, Angela Woodruff, got a call from the police, informing her of her mother's death. Angela was stunned. As far as she knew, her mother had been in very good health, despite her advanced age. Angela immediately phoned Dr. Shipman for an explanation. The doctor was out, but he later phoned back and told Angela that her mother had died of old age. He was also at pains to stress that a postmortem was unnecessary because he had seen her shortly before her death. Lastly, he recommended to Angela that she should have her mother cremated.

Angela Woodruff ignored this last piece of advice and in keeping with her mother's wishes had her buried. Then, following the funeral, she received a disconcerting call from a firm of solicitors. They claimed to be holding a copy of Mrs. Grundy's last will and testament.

A solicitor herself, Angela had always handled her mother's legal affairs and as far as she knew her firm held the original document. She therefore set up a meeting to view the new will. The moment she saw the poorly worded, poorly typed document, she knew that it was a fake. "My mother was a meticulously tidy person," she later testified, "the thought of her signing a document which is so badly typed didn't make any sense."

But the shoddy composition of the document was not the only concern. The new will bequeathed all of Kathleen Grundy's worldly possessions to her physician, Dr. Harold Shipman. Angela knew that her mother had liked and respected Shipman, but she could not understand why she'd have left her entire estate to him. She began to suspect that someone had drawn up the document in order to frame the doctor for Kathleen's death. However, after interviewing the two witnesses to the will, she reluctantly came to the conclusion that Dr. Shipman had murdered her mother for money. It was then that she took her suspicions to the police.

The case landed on the desk of Detective Superintendent Bernard Postles, and he quickly drew the same conclusion as Angela Woodruff. The will was quite obviously a forgery, and a crude one at that. It cast suspicion on the doctor, especially since Mrs. Grundy had died so soon after bequeathing her estate to him.

However, in order to prove murder, a postmortem would have to be carried out. An exhumation order was therefore obtained and hair and tissue samples were taken from the deceased and sent to different labs for analysis.

The police, meanwhile, were concerned that Dr. Shipman might hear of the exhumation and be scared into destroying evidence. They therefore launched a raid on the doctor's home and offices, logging into evidence a number of medical documents and an old typewriter, which would later prove to have been used to type the fake will.

Then the toxicology report arrived, and the police were in for a shock. They had expected that the doctor, with his medical knowledge, would have used a poison that would be difficult to trace - insulin, perhaps, which the body produces naturally. Instead, Shipman had injected Mrs. Grundy with a massive dose of morphine, one of the easiest toxins to detect. It pointed to someone confident in his ability to avoid detection, someone perhaps, who'd gotten away with this sort of thing before. Postles began to fear that Kathleen Grundy was not Dr. Shipman's only victim. He'd soon be proven devastatingly correct in that assumption.

Harold Frederick Shipman was born in Nottingham on January 14, 1946, the middle of three children. His mother, Vera, doted on him and kept a very strict rein on who Freddy (as he was affectionately called) was allowed to associate with. As a young boy, he did exceptionally well at school, although as he grew older his academic performance dropped off somewhat. In 1963, when he was 17 years old, Shipman's beloved mother died of lung cancer. She was only 43 at the time, and Shipman nursed her through her final months.

In 1965, Shipman went to study medicine at Leeds University, graduating in 1970. He then served an internship at Pontefract General Infirmary before entering work as a GP at a practice in Todmorden. By now, Shipman was already married and the father of two young children. He also proved to be an excellent GP, respected and well liked by staff and patients. Yet there was another side to Shipman. He could be confrontational, combative and rude. At times, he humiliated people and was fond of referring to those who disagreed with him as "stupid." He also insisted on having things done his way, even overruling the more experienced doctors in the practice.

Shipman had only been at Todmorden for two years when his career came to an abrupt halt. He began suffering blackouts, which he self-diagnosed as epilepsy. The truth was rather more sinister. Shipman had become addicted to the morphine-like drug pethidine and had been making out fraudulent prescriptions to obtain his fix. When this was discovered, he was fired from his job and charged with fraud and forgery. The penalty was ridiculously lenient – a £600 fine.

Although the General Medical Council did not see fit to strike him off, Shipman was barred from working in any capacity that gave him access to drugs. When this censure expired in 1977, he re-emerged as a GP in Hyde.

As he had at Todmorden, Shipman quickly established himself as a valuable member of staff. His new colleagues at the Donnybrook Surgery respected his work, while the patients loved his friendly bedside manner, even if he could be arrogant and patronizing at times. In 1992, he split from the Donnybrook practice to set up on his own, just around the corner on Market Street. He took with him a large list of patients.

Over the next five years, Shipman built up a steady practice of loyal patients, many of them elderly. However, by 1997, the first suspicions had begun to emerge about Shipman. The staff at Massey's, a local funeral parlor, had begun to notice similarities in many of the deceased that were sent to them for burial. Although all were elderly women, most of them were known to have been in good health immediately prior to their deaths. All had lived alone and all were found fully dressed, sitting in a chair or lying on a couch. If that wasn't enough of a coincidence, all had either been found dead by Dr. Shipman or had been visited by him shortly before they died.

At the same time, doctors at the Brooke Surgery, just over the road from Shipman, were becoming concerned about the number of deaths at his practice. Both they, and the directors of Massey's, passed on their concerns to the authorities. However, a covert examination of Shipman's records found no evidence of wrongdoing, and the authorities declined to take the matter further.

Now though, the police had every reason to investigate. Before long, fifteen bodies had been exhumed and Shipman found himself charged with multiple counts of murder.

The sheer scale of Shipman's killing spree is astonishing. The first murder was believed to have occurred on March 6, 1995, when Shipman injected Marie West with diamorphine. He attributed her death to a stroke.

Sixteen months later, on July 11, 1996, Shipman visited Irene Turner at her home. Mrs. Turner had recently returned from a holiday and had a cold, for which Shipman administered an injection. The syringe contained morphine and Mrs. Turner died soon after. He listed cause of death as diabetes.

On February 28, 1997, a friend of 77-year-old Lizzie Adams arrived for a visit and found Shipman at Ms. Adams' home and her friend sprawled out on the couch. Shipman claimed that he'd found Ms. Adams in this condition and had just called an ambulance. Then he pretended to make another call canceling the ambulance, saying that the patient had died. Phone records show that neither call was actually made. Shipman recorded cause of death as pneumonia.

On April 25, 1997, Shipman called on Jean Lilley. When a neighbor saw him leave she went to check on her friend and found her dead. Shipman claimed that the 59-year-old had died of heart failure, but a pathologist later found cause of death to be morphine poisoning.

The next to die was 63-year-old Ivy Lomas, killed at Shipman's surgery on May 29, 1997. Two days later, Shipman altered her medical records to fit in with his diagnosis. Mrs. Lomas was a regular at his surgery and Shipman often referred to her as a nuisance when talking to his staff.

Muriel Grimshaw was found dead at her home on July 14, 1997. Shipman claimed she'd died of a stroke, caused by hypertension. He then altered her medical records to support his diagnosis.

On November 28, 1997, Shipman killed Marie Quinn with an injection of morphine. He claimed that Mrs. Quinn had called him saying that she'd just suffered a stroke. He'd rushed to her home, but she was dead when he arrived. Phone records show no calls by Mrs. Quinn to Shipman's surgery on the day in question.

Shipman's next victim was Kathleen Wagstaff, who he claimed had summoned him to her home on December 9, 1997. Records show that no such call was made. He said she died of heart disease, but no evidence was found of any such illness.

Bianka Pomfret died at her home on December 10, 1997, shortly after a visit from Shipman. He claimed she had died of coronary thrombosis. Forensic experts later found that Shipman had altered the patient's medical records in order to create a backdated history of heart problems.

Norah Nuttall was visited by Shipman on January 26, 1998. Less than an hour later, her son arrived to find his mother dead in a chair. Shipman said he had called an ambulance, then canceled it when he realized that Mrs. Nuttall was dead. Phone records showed that neither call was made.

Pamela Hillier, an active 68-year-old, was found dead on February 9, 1998. Shipman said she'd died of a massive stroke. It was later proven that he'd made ten changes to her medical records in order to support his diagnosis.

Maureen Ward, 57, had been suffering from cancer but was in remission at the time of her death on February 18, 1998. Shipman recorded her cause of death as a brain tumor, then altered her medical records to suggest that the cancer had spread to her brain. A cancer specialist testified at trial that this was not the case and that Mrs. Ward had died from a massive overdose of diamorphine.

Winifred Mellor, 73, was found dead on May 11, 1998, having been visited by Shipman earlier in the day. He claimed she had died of coronary thrombosis and altered her medical records to make it look like she had been complaining of chest pains.

Joan Melia, 73, visited Shipman's surgery on June 12, 1998, suffering from a chest infection. Later that same day, he called at her home and claims to have found her dead. He issued a death certificate citing pneumonia aggravated by emphysema. A pathologist later found evidence of morphine but no serious lung problems.

And then there was Kathleen Grundy. Shipman had visited her early on the day of her death to take a blood sample, ostensibly for a study on aging. Unlike in the other murders, Shipman tried to profit from the crime with his falsified will. It was to prove his undoing.

Harold Shipman went on trial at the Preston Crown Court on October 5, 1999. The evidence against him was overwhelming and throughout the trial, he was caught in several lies. Yet he maintained his innocence to the end, offering up any number of ludicrous explanations for his actions.

The jury wasn't convinced. On the 31st January 2000, after six days of deliberation, they found Shipman guilty of fifteen counts of murder and one of forgery. He was sentenced to fifteen consecutive life terms, with the recommendation that he should never be released.

Harold Shipman, Britain's most prolific serial killer, was behind bars. Yet two questions remained: How many did Shipman kill, and why did he do it?

The answers will likely never be known. However, a public inquiry, chaired by High Court Judge, Dame Janet Smith, put the number of victims at 215 (171 women and 44 men, ranging in age from 41 to 93). Another investigation, conducted by University of Leicester professor Richard Baker, determined that Shipman killed at least 236 of his patients. Either of those numbers makes Shipman the most prolific serial killer in history.

As to why he did it, many contradictory theories have been suggested. Some psychoanalysts speculate that he hated older women; others feel he was re-creating his mother's death in order to satisfy some deep masochistic need. Still others suggest that he considered himself superior to other people and believed he could do whatever he wanted without fear of discovery. Another theory is that he was fighting a compulsion he simply could not control, and that the poorly forged will indicates he desperately wanted to be caught.

An element of truth probably exists in each of these explanations, but perhaps prosecutor Richard Henriques got closest to the answer when he said:

"He was exercising the ultimate power of controlling life and death, and repeated the act so often he must have found the drama of taking life to his taste."

We shall never know the whole truth. At around 6 a.m. on Tuesday, January 13, 2004, Harold Shipman was found hanging in his cell at Wakefield prison. He'd committed suicide by fashioning a noose from a bed sheet.

Miyuki Ishikawa

Miyuki Ishikawa is virtually unknown outside of her native Japan. Yet the "Demon Midwife" is the worst mass murder in Japanese history, responsible for the deaths of at least 103 infants. Even more chilling was her method of murder. She deliberately neglected the helpless babies in her care, allowing them to die a slow and painful death while she tried to extort money from their impoverished parents for services rendered.

Ishikawa was born in Kunitomi, Miyazaki Prefecture in 1897 and went on to study medicine at Tokyo University. Specializing as a midwife, she took up a position at Kotobuki Maternity Hospital, eventually working her way up to become director of the facility. During this time, she also married, although the union produced no children.

Ishikawa, at any rate, had her hands full with the running of her hospital, which was overcrowded and poorly funded. The women who gave birth here were, in the main, peasant stock with very little money and usually with many mouths to feed. Many of the children were simply abandoned at the hospital after the mothers gave birth.

For a time, Ishikawa sought genuinely to help, approaching social services and various charities for funding. When those requests were turned down, she settled on another solution, one as efficient as it was cruel and heartless. She turned to mass infanticide.

It is difficult to understand how someone trained in the care of newborns could carry out such atrocities, but Ishikawa appeared to believe that she was doing good. Her M.O. was to section off certain newborns, those from the most impoverished families, and leave them without care or sustenance until they died of hunger and thirst. The cries of these starving infants must have been horrendous to hear, but Ishikawa paid them no heed and instructed her staff to do the same. Many resigned in protest, although amazingly no one went to the authorities. To add insult to injury, Ishikawa sought to profit from these deaths. She approached the families of the dead children and demanded payment of around 4,000 yen. Her reasoning was that the amount was a pittance compared to the cost of raising a child.

Ishikawa went to great lengths to cover her tracks, paying off a doctor named Shiro Nakayama to issue fake death certificates, and paying bribes to various officials.

But the deaths of so many children could not go unnoticed forever, even in a country like Japan where at the time children were considered the "property" of their parents. Eventually, two police officers chanced upon five tiny boxes that were found to contain the emaciated corpses of five infants. It was quite obvious that the babies had not died of natural causes and an enquiry was launched.

First the carpenter who had constructed the boxes was traced. He said that he had built the tiny coffins, and many more like them, for the Kotobuki hospital. He also revealed that he had been taking the boxes to a local crematorium when the police had stopped him, a trip he'd made many times before.

The tiny corpses had meanwhile been removed to a local hospital for autopsy, where it was revealed that most had died of malnourishment and that some also showed signs of pneumonia. The deaths, in the view of the medical examiner, had been deliberately caused. The culprits were not difficult to find. On January 15, 1948, Miyuki Ishikawa was arrested along with her husband and accomplice, Takeshi.

With the suspects now in custody, the police expanded their investigation and recovered 70 more corpses scattered across various locations in Shinjuku district, including 30 buried at a local temple. Ishikawa meanwhile, was defiant, passing the blame on to irresponsible parents for having children that they could not afford to raise. Surprisingly, given the horrific nature of the crimes, public opinion appeared to be on her side.

That argument, however, was never going to hold up in a court of law. Yet even though she was found guilty of infanticide, the sentence was a ludicrously lenient eight years. Her husband and Dr. Nakayama got just four years in prison, and even those sentences were later halved by the Tokyo Superior Court in 1952.

And so it was, that Miyuki Ishikawa, the worst mass murderer in Japanese history, served only four years four the murder of over 100 infants. The case did, however, produce some positive outcomes, with new child protection laws passed and a new national certification system for midwives put in place. As a direct result of the Ishikawa case, Japan also passed a law legalizing abortions for financial reasons.

As for matron Ishikawa, little is known of her life after her release from prison.

Richard Angelo

He was an Eagle Scout as a boy and a volunteer fireman as soon as he was old enough to sign up. Friends and neighbors admired him, praising his diligence, devotion to duty and "can do" attitude. Students at his high school voted him, "most likely to succeed." Yet these words of praise sounded hollow to Richard Angelo, these tributes did little to address the festering feelings of worthlessness that he hid behind his upbeat façade. Instead, they instilled in him a desperate and obsessive need for recognition – an obsession that would ultimately have tragic results for the patients of Good Samaritan Hospital in West Islip, New York.

Richard Angelo was born April 29, 1962, in New York. He finished high school in 1980, thereafter embarking on a course of study that saw him graduate from New York State University in May 1985. There was never any doubt as to his career path after that. Richard wanted to help people, and he saw nursing as the best way to do that. Happily, his ambition was soon recognized. He worked for short spells at a couple of Long Island hospices before gaining permanent employment at the Good Samaritan Hospital in April 1987. There he was assigned to the night shift, tending intensive care patients.

As he'd done throughout his life, Angelo quickly impressed his colleagues and superiors with his work ethic and pleasant demeanor. He expressed no qualms about working the dreaded 11 p.m. to 7 a.m. stretch. In fact, he confided in his work colleagues that he actually preferred it.

All went well until the latter months of 1987 when doctors at Good Samaritan started picking up some worrying patterns in the ICU. Patients who had appeared to be recovering well from surgery were suddenly deteriorating and dying for no apparent reason. Hospital administrators were both perplexed and alarmed, especially when the rate accelerated between September and October. In the space of just under a month, there were six suspicious deaths in the ICU. It was beyond comprehension.

The mystery went some way towards unraveling itself on October 11, 1987. It had been a particularly traumatic day on the Intensive Care ward, with two patients dying after undergoing operations. The nursing staff was on high alert. Then, at around 11:30 in the evening, post-op patient Girolamo Cucich buzzed for a nurse. She arrived to find him clawing at his throat and struggling for breath, but quick action was fortunately enough to save his life. With his condition stabilized, Cucich told the nurse what had happened. He said that he'd been lying awake in bed when a bearded, heavyset man had entered his room. The man had been dressed in a hospital uniform, and Cucich had assumed that he was on the nursing staff. "I'm going to make you feel better," the man had told him, before injecting something into his I.V. tube. Almost immediately, Cucich experienced numbness and felt his chest constrict. Drawing on his last reserves of strength, he'd pressed the buzzer to summon a nurse. That action had saved his life.

The initial assumption was that the bearded stranger was someone from outside who had gained entrance to the hospital by posing as a nurse. But as police began questioning hospital workers on October 12, they couldn't help noticing that Richard Angelo was an almost exact match for the man described by Cucich. They, therefore, focused their attention on him, asking him directly if he'd injected the patient.

Angelo appeared outraged at the suggestion, but tests on the patient's urine soon confirmed that something had indeed been injected into his IV. Lab tests turned up traces of Pavulon, a drug that produces muscular paralysis. The police then obtained a warrant for Angelo's locker and turned up a treasure trove of evidence, including hypodermic needles and a vial of potassium chloride. This drug can induce a heart attack if misused and Angelo was not authorized to have it in his possession.

And yet Angelo still protested his innocence. On November 14, while he was out of town attending a conference for emergency medical technicians, detectives raided his apartment and found the evidence they needed - vials of Pavulon and Anectine (a similar drug). Angelo was arrested the next day.

Faced with the evidence against him, Richard Angelo finally broke down and confessed to injecting, at least, two patients per week with Pavulon or Anectine. Asked why he'd done it, Angelo told investigators: "I wanted to create a situation where I would cause the patient to have some respiratory distress or some problem, and through my intervention or suggested intervention or whatever, come out looking like I knew what I was doing. I had no confidence in myself. I felt very inadequate."

The only problem with this plan was that, more often than not, Angelo was not able to save the patient. In his last six weeks on the job, there were 37 "Code Blue" emergencies, during which 25 patients died. A conservative estimate put the number of Angelo's victims at 38.

Richard Angelo would eventually be found guilty of two counts of second-degree murder, plus one count each of manslaughter and criminally negligent homicide. Psychologists testified at his trial that he suffered from dissociative identity disorder and that after injecting his victims, he moved into a separate personality that made him unaware of what he had just done. This, however, did not preclude him from responsibility for his actions. He was sentenced to life in prison.

Richard Angelo is currently incarcerated at Clinton Correctional Facility in Dannemora, New York.

Marcel Petiot

On the morning of March 6, 1944, residents of the upper-class Rue le Sueur in Paris, France phoned the police to complain about foul smoke issuing from the chimney at number 21. It had been going on for days they protested, and when they'd gone to complain to the owner, Dr. Marcel Petiot, they'd found he wasn't at home. A note pinned to the door of the luxury three-story villa informed them that he'd be away for the rest of the month.

The police officers soon learned that Petiot maintained another residence, two miles away at 66 Rue Caumartin. A telephone call found the doctor at home. "Don't do anything," he cautioned. "I'll be there in 15 minutes."

Half an hour later, Petiot still hadn't shown, and with the smoke worsening and the street filling with onlookers, the gendarmes decided it was time to call the fire brigade.

There was still no sign of Petiot by the time the firefighters arrived. Entering the building through a second-story window, two firemen began searching for the source of the conflagration. A short while later they staggered from the house, visibly shaken. One of them stooped over and threw up in the garden. The other approached the police officers and told them what he and his colleague had found.

Three officers then entered the building. Following the firefighter's instructions, they headed directly for the basement. The first thing they noticed was the stench of seared flesh. Its source was soon obvious. A large iron stove blazed away in one corner, a human arm dangling from its open door. Nearby stood a pile of coal and beside it a stack of dismembered human corpses.

Stunned by the grisly display, the officers staggered from the basement just as Dr. Petiot arrived on his bicycle. Petiot immediately called them into a huddle and dropped his voice. "This is serious," he whispered. "My head could be at stake."

After questioning each of the cops to ascertain that he was a "loyal Frenchman," Petiot explained that he was the leader of a Resistance cell and that the bodies in his cellar were of Germans and collaborators. He insisted that he had over 300 confidential files at his home that needed to be destroyed, lest they fall into the hands of the Gestapo. Convinced by Petiot's apparent sincerity, the gendarmes let him go. It would be seven months before they eventually caught up with him again.

Marcel André Henri Félix Petiot was born on January 17, 1897, in Auxerre, France. Later accounts of his childhood paint him as a malevolent individual who displayed all the signs of the fledgling serial killer, including animal cruelty, bed-wetting and a precocious interest in sex. However, it is unclear if these were invented later, to fit the crimes he committed. What we do know is that Petiot was a troublemaker, that he was expelled from school several times, and that he was diagnosed as mentally ill at age 17.

During World War I, Petiot served with the French infantry and was wounded in action as well as suffering the effects of mustard gas. He was also diagnosed with various mental ailments and eventually discharged with a full disability pension.

At the conclusion of the war, Petiot entered the accelerated education program available to veterans, completing a medical degree in just eight months. He then served a two-year internship at Evreux Mental Hospital, receiving his medical degree in December of 1921. Amazing though it seems, the former juvenile delinquent and mental patient was now a qualified physician.

Petiot moved next to the small town of Villeneuve-sur-Yonne, where he set up a practice and quickly gained an unsavory reputation for performing illegal abortions and supplying narcotics to drug addicts. Despite this, he built up a thriving practice with many loyal patients who would not hear a bad word spoken about him.

In 1926, Petiot began an affair with Louise Delaveau, the young daughter of one of his patients. When Louise disappeared in May

1926, neighbors reported that they had seen Petiot loading a trunk into his car in the dead of night. Just such a trunk was retrieved from a local river months later, containing the dismembered remains of a young woman. Decomposition made a positive identification impossible, but despite strong suspicion that this was the missing Louise, Petiot was never charged. That same year, Petiot decided to enter politics and was elected mayor of Villeneuve-sur-Yonne. Once in office, he quickly set about embezzling town funds.

In 1927, Mayor Petiot married the daughter of a wealthy landowner. The following year he fathered a son. By then, the town was already awash with rumors of Petiot helping himself to public funds and assets. Still, he managed to hang on to his position until August 1931, when matters eventually came to a head and he was suspended as mayor. Barely skipping a beat, Petiot resigned his position and aimed higher, standing as councilor for the Yonne district. Elected despite the rumors circling around him, Petiot was immediately back to his old tricks. He was eventually dismissed for embezzlement and for the theft of electricity. By then, he had already decamped for Paris.

As he'd done in Villeneuve-sur-Yonne, Petiot quickly built up a roster of loyal patients in the capital. Just as quickly, he acquired a reputation for shady practices, abortions, drug dealing, and theft. In 1936, he applied for and was granted, a designation that gave him the authority to issue death certificates. That same year, he spent time in an institution after being diagnosed with kleptomania.

World War II arrived two years later, bringing disaster to France and all of Europe. To a man like Marcel Petiot though, it presented nothing but opportunity. He had soon hatched a quite horrific murder-for-profit scheme, laying the groundwork by posing as a member of the Resistance. Petiot gave credence to his claims by spreading tall tales about his exploits. He claimed to have developed a weapon that killed Germans without leaving any trace, he boasted about his meetings with high-level Allied commanders and hinted that he was secretly working with a group of Spanish anti-fascist fighters.

In 1941, Petiot recruited three accomplices – Raoul Fourrier, Edmond Pintard, and René-Gustave Nézondet – and began putting the word out that he was operating an escape route, code name "Fly-Tox," for those wanting to flee occupied France. For a price of 25,000 Francs, Petiot promised that he could smuggle anyone out of the country to Argentina, via Portugal.

It was, of course, a scam. Desperate people, most of them from wealthy Jewish families, would pay the 25,000 Franc fee and arrive at Petiot's premises at 21 rue le Sueur laden with cash, jewelry, furs, and other valuables, ready to flee the country. Petiot would inform them that they required an inoculation before being allowed to enter Argentina. He himself would deliver the shot, all included in the price, of course. But the "inoculation" he administered was usually cyanide, which sent his victims to a swift and unceremonious death. In other cases, Petiot used slower-acting drugs and took pleasure in watching the death throes of his victims through a peephole in a purpose-built chamber.

With the victims dispatched, Petiot would then take possession of their valuables and dispose of the bodies. At first, he simply instructed his accomplices to dump them in the Seine. But when the number of corpses being pulled from the river aroused suspicion, he changed his disposal method to submersion in quicklime, and later to incineration.

But Petiot soon had another problem to contend with. He had been less than discreet in advertising his services and, in April 1943, the Gestapo began hearing rumors of the Fly-Tox escape route. Keen to infiltrate the operation, they sent a Jewish prisoner named Yvan Dreyfus to approach the network. He promptly disappeared.

Undeterred, the Gestapo tried again and, this time, succeeded in arresting Petiot confederates Fourrier, Pintard, and Nézondet. Under torture, they quickly gave up "Dr. Eugène" and Petiot was taken into custody. He would remain a prisoner of the Gestapo for eight months, until January 1944.

You might think that, with the Gestapo breathing down his neck, Dr. Petiot would have scaled back his murder-for-profit operation. But no sooner had he been released from custody than he was back advertising his escape route. His period in Gestapo captivity had, of course, bolstered his Resistance credentials, and with the Nazi's stepping up the deportation of Jews to the labor camps in Poland, there was more demand than ever. Soon hapless would-be refugees were streaming to his door and Petiot was cashing in. It led eventually to that fateful morning in March when the police were called to Petiot's villa. Now, however, the doctor was gone, and a search of his home at 21 Rue le Sueur, produced evidence of mass murder, with enough body parts discovered to make "at least ten complete bodies."

But still the police wavered, uncertain whether Petiot was, in fact, a murderer, or the hero of the Resistance he claimed to be. It was the Gestapo who inadvertently swung things in Petiot's favor. After they labeled him a "dangerous lunatic" and issued a warrant for his arrest, the French police backed down. They were not about to do the Nazis' dirty work for them.

Petiot meanwhile, was nowhere to be found. Over the next seven months, he hid with friends and loyal former patients. He grew a beard and adopted various aliases.

But the tide of war was turning. In August, the Resistance and the Paris police staged an uprising against the Germans in Paris and by the following month, the capital had been liberated. This, of course, was not good news for Petiot, but he responded with typical gall. Emerging from hiding, he adopted the name "Henri Valeri" and joined the newly formed French Forces of the Interior (FFI). He was made a captain and put in charge of counterespionage and prisoner interrogations, charged with rooting out collaborators. One of the top names on his list was Marcel Petiot, whose Resistance credentials had been disclaimed and was now being sought as a common murderer.

In September 1946, the newspaper 'Resistance' published a scathing article about Petiot, naming him not only as a murderer but also a collaborator and a "soldier of the Reich." Petiot was enraged by the accusations, so much so that he wrote a letter to his former attorney describing the newspaper article as "filthy kraut lies." It was an ill-judged move. All that the letter achieved was to prove to the FFI that Petiot was still in Paris. They stepped up their search for him, with Captain Henri Valéri at the forefront of the action.

In the end though, it was not the FFI who tracked down Petiot, but an ordinary citizen. On the morning of October 31, Petiot was recognized by one of his former patients at a Paris metro station. She pointed him out to a police officer and he was arrested on the spot. He was found to have 31,700 Francs in cash, and 50 identity documents, issued in six different names. The police, it seemed, had caught him just in time.

Marcel Petiot eventually went on trial on March 19, 1946. Faced with 135 criminal charges, he stuck steadfastly to his story that he had only killed enemies of France and was a hero of the Resistance. This declaration was not helped by the fact that no Resistance member could be found who actually knew Petiot, nor that the cells he claimed to have been a member of, were fictitious.

As for the families that he claimed to have ferried safely to South America, not one could be found. All evidence suggested that they'd entered Rue le Sueur and had never been seen alive again. The court was also interested to know why they would have departed for Argentina leaving their clothes, valuables, passports and other property in Petiot's possession. To this, the doctor could offer no viable answer.

In the end, Petiot's tales about his heroics in the Resistance were exposed as an elaborate lie, concocted to conceal the murders of at least 60 individuals. Petiot was found guilty on 26 counts and sentenced to death.

Marcel Petiot went to the guillotine on May 25, 1946. To his credit, the worst mass murderer in France's history walked unflinchingly to his death, even joking with his jailers in the moments before the blade fell.

Kimberly Saenz

Medical serial killers commit murder for a variety of reasons. Harold Shipman killed because he enjoyed the godlike power of life and death he had over his patients; Genene Jones killed because she became addicted to the exhilaration of dealing with "Code Blue" situations; Charles Cullen killed out of frustration with his life, which appeared to be spiraling out of control.

And then there is Kimberly Saenz. Like many of the medical serial killers featured in this volume, Saenz's life had started out as one of promise. At high school, she'd been a cheerleader and a talented softball player, a popular girl with lots of friends. Then, in her senior year, she became pregnant and had to drop out. Still, she made the best of a bad situation. She married the father of her child and was, by all accounts, a good parent. She also enrolled in nursing college and emerged with an LPN (Licensed Practical Nurse) qualification. Her first employer had nothing but praise for

Saenz, describing her as "a compassionate, caring individual who assisted her patients and was well liked."

But then something happened that would turn Kimberly Saenz's life upside down. She became addicted to prescription drugs, most of them pilfered from the hospitals where she worked.

In quick succession, Saenz lost four health care jobs, usually for stealing prescription medications. At the same time, she stopped caring about her appearance, began putting on weight, started having problems in her marriage. Her husband, Mark, filed for divorce and had to obtain a restraining order against her in 2007 after she arrived at his home drunk and abusive. That same incident saw her arrested for public intoxication and for criminal trespass.

And yet, despite her obviously troubled mental state, Saenz continued to work in the healthcare industry. In June 2007, she was fired from Woodland Heights Hospital for stealing Demerol, a powerful painkiller. Two months later, she got a job at DaVita Dialysis clinic in Lufkin, about 125 miles northeast of Houston, Texas.

In April 2008, a Lufkin fire official wrote anonymously to state health inspectors, urging them to investigate the DaVita Clinic, due to the unusually high number of paramedic calls being logged from that location, 16 in the first two weeks of April alone.

Inspectors were duly dispatched, arriving within days of the initial report. They were stunned at what they found. The fire official had understated the case somewhat. During the month of April, paramedics had been called to DaVita on no fewer than thirty occasions (compared to just twice during the previous year and a half). And despite the quick response of emergency medics, patients had died, four in April alone, with seven more having to be resuscitated after suffering cardiac problems. Something was clearly wrong and inspectors soon found a common thread. In 84 percent of the cases, the attending nurse had been Kimberly Saenz.

At 4:30 a.m. on April 28, 2008, Saenz arrived for work and was told by her supervisor, Amy Clinton, that she was being taken off her dialysis shift for the day and was required to work as a patient care technician.

Saenz was visibly distressed at the news, which meant that she would be cleaning up after patients, rather than giving out medication, as she was used to. She was actually in tears as she went around the wards with her mop and bucket.

At around 6 a.m., patients Marva Rhone and Carolyn Risinger arrived at the clinic for their dialysis treatment. A short while later, two other patients reported something disturbing. They said that they had seen Saenz pour bleach into her bucket, fill a syringe with the caustic liquid, and then inject it into the I.V. lines of Rhone and Risinger.

Thankfully, neither of the women went into cardiac arrest, although tests revealed the presence of sodium hypochlorite (bleach) in their I.V. lines. Sainz was then called in and fired from her job. It would take nearly a year, and a protracted investigation, before she was placed under arrest on April 1, 2009.

Kimberly Saenz went on trial in 2012, charged with the murders of five patients – Clara Strange, Thelma Metcalf, Garlin Kelley, Cora Bryant, and Opal Few. With the possibility of a death penalty hanging over his client's head, defense attorney T. Ryan Deaton sought to shift the blame. He described Saenz as a scapegoat, who was being used to cover up the poor procedures in place at the DaVita Clinic, which were the actual reason for the deaths. "What possible motive did my client have for killing these people?" Deaton asked the jury.

Angelina County District Attorney Clyde Herrington was only too happy to address that question. He described Saenz as a depressed and disgruntled employee who complained constantly about specific patients, including some of those who had been killed. Saenz had substance abuse problems, had been fired from at least four health care jobs and had seen her marriage disintegrate. Frustrated and angry at her situation she'd struck out, targeting the most helpless of victims, the sick people under her care.

In the end, the evidence against Kimberly Saenz was just too strong for the jury to ignore. She was found guilty of five counts of murder (although it was suspected that she'd actually killed at least five more) and was sentenced to life in prison without the possibility of parole. She is currently incarcerated at the Dr. Lane Murray Unit, a women's prison in Gatesville, Texas.

Stephan Letter

An unmarked van rolls to a stop outside the cemetery gates in the picturesque Alpine town of Sonthofen, Germany. Six hooded figures emerge, all dressed in white biological suits. Stepping like lunar astronauts they enter the cemetery and start walking towards a nearby gravesite where a mini-excavator is piling up a small mound of earth. A team of laborers stands by with ropes and pulleys, ready to bring the coffin to the surface. As the forensic team approaches, they can see that the casket has just been exposed. It is one of 42 that will be hauled up during the coming days, one of 42 autopsies that pathologists will need to perform. All are suspected victims of Stephan Letter, Germany's worst serial killer since the war.

As a boy, Stephan Letter was always interested in pursuing a medical career. His first ambition had been to qualify as an ER doctor, but mediocre academic results meant that he'd had to abandon that dream and settle for nursing instead. Not that it appeared to bother Stephan. So keen was he to begin serving those in need that he volunteered at the Red Cross while still attending nursing college in Ludwigsburg.

One of Letter's jobs at the Red Cross had been to drive elderly patients from their homes to a clinic for treatment. Those who worked with Letter during this time described him as compassionate and caring, although prone to lapses of professionalism and shows of emotion. He would become extremely distressed by the sickly condition of his frail charges. In January 2003, having graduated from Ludwigsburg, he finally had the chance to start doing something to help.

Letter's first posting was to the Sonthofen Clinic, a hospital in the idyllic mountainside village of Sonthofen, in Bavaria. He started working there shortly after his graduation, pulling the night shift. A competent and diligent worker, Letter seemed to genuinely care about his elderly patients. Perhaps he cared too much, for their suffering appeared to affect him on a deeply personal level.

Within a month of Letter beginning his career at Sonthofen, there was a marked upswing in the number of deaths at the hospital. Yet, as most of the deceased patients were over 75 years of age, the deaths caused little alarm. Even when two younger patients, aged 40 and 47, died suddenly, no alarms were triggered. Both patients had been gravely ill and their deaths were not entirely unexpected.

But there were other deaths that should have raised a red flag. Beata Giehl, 79, was taken to the Sonthofen Clinic on April 30,

2003, having suffered a suspected heart attack. She responded well to treatment and by that afternoon was sitting up in bed, laughing and chatting with her daughters. By 10 o'clock that evening she had passed away.

And then there was Pilar Del Rio Peinador. The 73-year-old Spanish national had been admitted to the clinic with breathing problems but was recovering well and had been talking to hospital staff about a planned holiday to her homeland. Then one morning, having shown no deterioration in her condition, she was dead.

Cases such as this might well have alerted the attention of the authorities, but they didn't, and neither did the sudden escalation in the number of deaths at Sonthofen. When the case eventually broke it was not a suspicious death, but missing drugs, that pointed to the presence of a serial killer.

In July 2004, a hospital administrator called the police to report that stocks of a muscle-relaxing drug were missing. Investigators were somewhat bemused by the report since the medicines did not come under the dangerous drugs law. They were freely available for medical staff, both doctors and nurses, to use as required. However, when they heard of the quantities that had disappeared, their ears pricked up. Given in that quantity, the drug would almost certainly be lethal. And since the drug had no street value, it was almost certain that the thief had murder in mind.

Tracking down the culprit proved to be a relatively easy matter. Detectives compared the clinic's duty roster against the dates when the drugs had disappeared. The evidence pointed to one man – Stephan Letter. A subsequent search of his apartment turned up enough of the missing drug to have killed ten people.

Thus far, Letter was suspected of nothing more than theft of hospital property, but as the police began pressing him on why he'd stolen the tranquilizers, he suddenly blurted out that he had killed at least 16 patients, adding that, "there may be more."

Letter then went on to explain his motive. He said that the deaths were mercy killings, designed to release the patients from their suffering, to "release their souls," as he put it. He said that he would listen in as doctors discussed a patient's condition and determine whether they were likely to recover. If not, he'd administer a cocktail of tranquilizers and muscle relaxants during the night, to stop their breathing. Later, he'd alert a doctor to the patient's death. Often, he'd console grieving relatives.

The only problem with Letter's story was that many of his victims were recent admissions to the hospital, whose state of health had not even been properly diagnosed by the time he sent them to oblivion. It was Letter himself who was making the decision as to who lived or died, Letter who was playing God. Without his intervention, many of the victims would likely have made a full recovery.

Stephan Letter went on trial at the Bavarian state court in Kempten in December 2006. His mercy-killing defense exposed as a lie, he was convicted of 12 counts of murder, 15 of manslaughter, and one count of killing on demand. He was also found guilty of attempted manslaughter and of causing grievous bodily harm.

After the verdict was announced the 28-year-old Letter turned towards the public gallery where the relatives of many of his victims were seated. "Es Tut Mir Leid," he mouthed - I am sorry.

Letter was sentenced to life in prison. In a highly unusual move for Germany, the judge ruled that no upper limit should be placed on the life sentence, thus ensuring that Letter would not be released for good behavior after the mandatory 15 years.

Donald Harvey

Donald Harvey was born in Butler County, Ohio, in 1952. Shortly after his birth, his parents moved to Booneville, Kentucky, a small town in the foothills of the Appalachian Mountains. Donald was raised here, and grew up in a loving family environment. By all accounts, he was a happy, well-adjusted child, somewhat quiet, but always well behaved. At school, he was a diligent student who classmates remember as a bit of a loner. He took part in no extracurricular activities, preferring to spend his time reading.

In 1968, Harvey graduated to Booneville High School where he continued to excel academically. He routinely earned A's and B's on his report card, usually with little effort. It was, therefore, a surprise to his teachers when he dropped out without graduating.

After leaving school, Harvey relocated to Cincinnati, Ohio, where he got a job in a factory, continuing there until 1970, when he was laid off. A few days later, Harvey got a call from his mother asking him to visit his ailing grandfather at Marymount Hospital in London, Kentucky. At a loose end after losing his job, Harvey agreed. It would prove to be a fateful decision.

While Harvey was in Kentucky, he spent most of his time visiting with his grandfather. He was soon a fixture at the hospital, well known to most of the nuns who worked there and universally liked by them. During a conversation with one of the sisters, Harvey was asked if he'd be interested in working at Marymount as an orderly. He readily accepted, starting work the next day.

Although he had no medical training, some of Harvey's duties involved attending to patients – changing bedpans, inserting catheters and passing out medications. Harvey didn't mind, in fact, he kind of enjoyed helping ailing people. It gave him a feeling of power over them, and in some way that he didn't understand just yet, that thrilled him.

Like many serial killers, Donald Harvey committed his first murder on an impulse. It happened after he'd been at Marymount for only a couple of months. Harvey was working the evening shift and had gone to a private room to check on a stroke victim. As he was leaning over the bed to examine the patient's catheter, the man suddenly pulled his hand out from under the covers and shoved feces in Harvey's face. Harvey sprang back, but too late to avoid being smeared with the vile substance. To make matters worse, the patient laughed at his reaction.

Harvey responded angrily, pulling the pillow out from under the patient's head, placing it over his face and pushing down. He held the pillow in place until the man stopped struggling. Then he rearranged the scene and went to have a shower before notifying the nurses that the patient had died. He was terrified that he'd be caught, but no one suspected anything but natural causes. Afterwards, reflecting on the murder, Harvey felt a tremendous sense of peace. Just three weeks later, he killed again, disconnecting an elderly woman's oxygen tank. Again, no one suspected foul play.

Harvey had gotten away with two murders and he felt invincible. He understood now the sense of superiority he had over his patients. It was because he held the power of life and death over them. The act of murder had become a drug, more addictive than any narcotic. He embarked on a murder spree, killing patients by a variety of methods – suffocation with plastic bags, morphine injections, cocktails of various drugs. Within a year, he'd racked up a dozen victims.

If some of these murders were motivated by mercy, as he'd later insist, others were definitely provoked by anger. In one case, Harvey got into an argument with a patient. The man insisted that Harvey was trying to kill him, and swung a bedpan at him, knocking him out cold. Later that evening, Harvey crept into the patient's room and punctured the man's catheter with a coat hanger. Infection set in. Within a few days, the patient had died in agony.

But while Harvey may have been getting away with murder at the hospital, he was less adept at other criminal activities. On March 31, 1971, he was arrested for burglary. Harvey was drunk when he was brought in and under questioning began muttering about the murders he'd committed. Arresting officers were stunned and decided to delve deeper. They questioned Harvey extensively but decided that outside of his admissions there was no evidence to make a charge of murder stick.

A few weeks later, Harvey went on trial for burglary, pleaded guilty to the lesser charge of petty theft, and paid an admission of guilt fine. He also resigned his post at Marymount Hospital and joined the US Air Force.

Harvey served less than a year in the Air Force before receiving a general discharge in March 1972. The grounds for the discharge were not stated, but it was rumored that his superiors were informed of his murder confession to the Kentucky police. His dismissal from the military brought on bouts of depression and in July 1972, Harvey checked into the Veteran's Administration Medical Center in Lexington, Kentucky. He would be in and out of the mental ward of that facility over the next six months.

In August, following a bungled suicide attempt, Harvey was placed in restraints and received electroshock therapy. In October, he was discharged. His mother would later condemn the hospital for releasing her son when he clearly still needed help.

Harvey spent the next few months getting his life back together, eventually finding part-time work as a nurse's aide at Cardinal Hill Hospital in Lexington. In June 1973, he got a second nursing job at Lexington's Good Samaritan Hospital. He worked both jobs until August 1974, when he took up a clerical post at St. Luke's Hospital in Fort Thomas, Kentucky.

Harvey would later claim that he was able to control his murderous urges during this period. This is a dubious assertion. Closer to the truth would be that he simply lacked contact with potential victims. Given the sort of access he had enjoyed at Marymount, he would almost certainly have resumed his murder spree. He needed a job where he could get close to patients. He found one back in Cincinnati.

In September 1975, Harvey found employment working the night shift at Cincinnati V.A. Medical Hospital. His duties were varied and included nursing assistant, housekeeping aide, cardiac-catheterization technician, and autopsy assistant. This suited the opportunistic serial killer down to the ground. Working nights meant he had very little supervision, and his varied job roster gave him access to virtually any area of the hospital. Harvey took full advantage.

Over the next 10 years, he would murder at least 15 patients, keeping a detailed diary of his crimes. He took meticulous notes on each victim, including the method he used to kill them. And his methods were as varied as they were sickening; pressing a plastic bag over the mouth and nose; rat poison in the patient's food; adding arsenic and cyanide to beverages; injecting cyanide into an intravenous tube or into a patient's buttocks.

While committing his crimes, Harvey studied medical journals and refined his techniques, all the while learning better ways of concealing his despicable acts. He also pilfered medical supplies, building up a vast stockpile of poisons and drugs. As the 80s arrived, he began to take greater risks. He started poisoning people that he knew.

The first to suffer these attentions was his gay lover, Carl Hoeweler. Harvey suspected that Hoeweler was cheating on him, and began putting small doses of arsenic into his food. The objective, Harvey would later claim, wasn't to kill. He merely wanted to make Hoeweler sick enough so he wouldn't be able to leave the apartment.

He exacted revenge on others too, and for any perceived slight. After an argument with one of his neighbors, he broke into her apartment and spiked her milk with hepatitis serum, nearly killing her. Another neighbor wasn't so lucky. Harvey poisoned her with arsenic. She died a week later.

After an argument with Hoeweler's parents in April 1983, Harvey started poisoning them too. He laced their food with arsenic, resulting in Hoeweler's father, Henry, suffering a stroke. While Henry was in the hospital, Harvey paid him a visit, dropping arsenic in his dessert before he left. Henry Hoeweler died later that night.

In January 1984, Carl Hoeweler called time on their relationship and asked Harvey to move out of his apartment. Harvey was enraged at the rejection and spent the next two years trying to kill Hoeweler with various poisons. He also tried, unsuccessfully, to murder a female acquaintance of Hoeweler.

Harvey's murder campaign suffered a setback on July 18, 1985. While leaving work, he was caught up in a routine search of his gym bag. The search turned up various items of contraband and a .38-caliber pistol. Harvey was fined $50 for carrying a firearm on hospital property. He was also given the option of resigning, rather than being fired. He took the option and walked away with a clean work record.

Seven months later, he was back in medical employment, this time as a part-time nurses' aide at Cincinnati's Drake Memorial Hospital. Before long, Harvey had earned a full-time position at Drake and he started killing again. Within just over a year, he'd killed another 23 patients - disconnecting life support machines, injecting air into their veins, suffocating them, injecting them with arsenic, cyanide, even drain cleaners.

In fact, so many patients died under Donald Harvey's care that he earned an ominous nickname around the hospital, "Angel of Death." Still, no one suspected anything was amiss until April 1987, and the murder of John Powell.

Powell had been in a coma for several months but had been showing signs of recovery when he died suddenly. During the autopsy, the coroner detected a faint scent of almonds, a telltale sign of cyanide poisoning. Tissue sample proved that the patient had, in fact, been poisoned, and an investigation was launched.

Having eliminated Powell's friends and family as suspects, the police began to focus on hospital employees, and once they heard of Donald Harvey's macabre nickname, and its origins, suspicion fell firmly on him.

Police obtained a search warrant for Harvey's apartment and turned up a mountain of evidence - large amounts of cyanide and arsenic, a library of books on various poisons, and most damningly, his detailed murder diary. Harvey was placed under arrest for one count of aggravated murder. He filed a plea of "not guilty by reason of insanity" and was held under a $200,000 bond.

Meanwhile, the police were beginning to look into several other suspicious deaths at the hospital. Realizing that the full extent of his crimes would soon be discovered, Harvey contacted investigators and offered a full confession in exchange for avoiding Ohio's death penalty.

Harvey began reciting his confession on August 11, eventually admitting to more than 70 murders over a 17-year period. Investigators were stunned by these numbers and insisted on a psychiatric evaluation by a panel of experts. A statement issued by the Cincinnati prosecutor's office best sums up their conclusion. "This man is sane, competent, but is a compulsive killer. He builds up tension in his body, so he kills people."

On August 18, 1987, Donald Harvey pled guilty to 24 counts of aggravated murder, four counts of attempted murder, and one count of felonious assault. He received four consecutive 20-years-to-life sentences.

Three weeks later, a Kentucky court sentenced him to eight life terms for the 12 murders committed at Marymount Hospital. In

February 1988, he entered guilty pleas on three additional Cincinnati homicides, drawing three more life sentences.

Donald Harvey will be eligible for parole in 2047, by which time he will be 95 years old.

Thomas Neill Cream

It was 1892, four years since the deadly psychopath, known only as Jack the Ripper, had killed the last of his five victims. The Ripper had not been forgotten, though, his horrendous crimes lived on in the memory, and speculations as to his identity were still a popular topic of conversation. Yet, even as the Ripper continued to cast his pall over London's East End, another ghoul appeared to prey on the city's streetwalkers. In many ways, this new fiend was more sadistic, more frightening, than the Ripper. Whereas Saucy Jack's kills were executed quickly, by strangulation or the flash of a blade, this brute's hapless victims were consigned to the agonizing death of strychnine poisoning. His name was Dr. Thomas Neill Cream. Some believe he may also have been the elusive Jack.

Thomas Neill Cream was born in Glasgow, Scotland, on May 27, 1850, the first of William and Mary Cream's eight children. Four years after his birth, the family immigrated to Canada and settled in Wolfe's Cove, Quebec. Here, William Cream found employment as a manager with Gilmour & Company, a shipbuilding and lumber firm. Years later, William used his acquired knowledge to start his own lumber business, which prospered. All of the Cream offspring followed their father into this trade, except Thomas who displayed little interest in commerce. An excellent student with a sharp intellect, Thomas decided early on that he wanted to be a doctor. He realized this ambition in April 1876, graduating from the reputable McGill University.

The ink had hardly dried on Cream's diploma when he was in trouble. During his internship, he'd been courting a teenaged girl by the name of Flora Brooks, the daughter of a wealthy hotel owner. When Flora became ill after a visit from Cream, a doctor was called and his examination determined that the young girl had recently had an abortion. The Brooks clan was enraged. They hunted Cream down and forced him to "do the right thing" and marry Flora. Left with no option, Cream went through with the nuptials. But he didn't stick around long. On the morning after the wedding, he was gone, fled to London, England.

Cream arrived in London in October 1876. As a foreign-qualified doctor, he was required to undergo certification before being allowed to practice medicine in Britain. To this extent he registered at St. Thomas' Hospital, in Lambeth, south London, to undergo further training. However, after six months of study, Cream failed to pass the entrance exam at the Royal College of Surgeons, due in the main to his extra-curricula activities. Cream spent more time escorting various society ladies around town than at his studies. He also enjoyed visiting the East End's many taverns, brothels, music halls and vaudeville theaters.

But if Cream wanted to earn a living as a doctor in Britain, he needed to buckle down and pass his examinations. He therefore removed himself from the temptations of London and relocated to Edinburgh where he received the requisite qualification from the Royal College of Physicians and Surgeons. Before departing London, though, Cream had had news from his homeland. His wife, Flora, had died, apparently of consumption. Later, a more sinister explanation would surface for Flora's untimely death. It would emerge that she'd died after swallowing some pills that her errant husband had sent her from England.

With certification in hand from the Royal College, Cream was now free to commence his medical career in Britain. However, for some inexplicable reason, he returned to Canada in late 1878 and set up practice in the bustling town of London, Ontario. The practice, on Dundas Street, quickly picked up a solid roster of patients and appeared to be doing well until it was embroiled in scandal. In May 1879, a patient named Kate Gardener was found dead in a shack behind the surgery. An examination revealed that the unmarried woman was pregnant at the time of her death, and it was surmised that she'd come to Dr. Cream for an abortion.

Under questioning, Cream admitted that that was indeed the case but insisted that he had refused to perform the operation. As the corpse had reeked of chloroform, he suggested that Gardner might have killed herself. The inquest, however, rejected that hypothesis and ruled the death a murder. The implication, of course, was that Cream was the culprit and although there was nothing to connect him with the crime, the scandal ruined both his reputation and his medical practice. Before long he'd absconded for Chicago.

Cream arrived in Illinois in August 1879, setting up business at 434 West Madison, conveniently close to the red light district. He quickly gained a reputation as an abortionist. In early 1880, he narrowly escaped jail time after a prostitute named Mary Anne Faulkner was found dead in a tenement flat, the result of a botched termination. Fortunately for Cream, his politically connected lawyer managed to get the charges dropped. He also got Cream off after another patient died as a result of taking one of his strychnine-laced anti-pregnancy pills.

In addition to his abortion business, Cream made a tidy sum from quack medicines. One of his most popular remedies was an elixir claiming to cure epilepsy. A number of patients swore by this treatment. One of them, a man named Daniel Stott, made the mistake of sending his attractive young wife to Cream's surgery for regular doses of the drug. Soon, Cream and Julia Stott were lovers and when her husband became suspicious of the affair, Cream doctored his medication with strychnine. Stott died on June 14, 1881, and Cream would likely have gotten away with the murder had it not been for his own paranoia.

Afraid that the cause of death might be discovered, Cream wrote a letter to the coroner, accusing the pharmacist of adding strychnine to his formula. The accusation was passed on to the district attorney who ordered Stott's body exhumed. As Cream had attested, large doses of strychnine were found in the man's stomach - but it was Cream, not the pharmacist, who was blamed. Hearing of a warrant for his arrest, he fled to Canada but was soon captured.

Cream was returned to Chicago to stand trial. And with Julia Stott turning state's evidence, he was found guilty of murder. In November 1881, he was sent to Joliet State Penitentiary for life. He'd spend a decade there before being paroled on July 21, 1891, thanks to his brother Daniel's political connections and a considerable sum of money to grease the palms of corrupt state officials.

Cream returned to Canada where a sizeable inheritance of $16,000, left at his father's passing, awaited. Ten years behind bars had taken its toll on the once handsome doctor. He looked older than his forty years, his head bald, skin weathered, eyes watery, yellowed and somewhat crossed. His once trim, square-shouldered build had drooped. He complained of throbbing headaches and spoke with an odd rattle. Prison had changed his attitude too, especially about women who he disparaged at every opportunity. His family was only too happy to bid him farewell when he departed Canada in September 1891 aboard the SS Teutonic bound for Liverpool.

Cream was back in London by October 1891, staying first at Anderson's Hotel on Fleet Street before moving to a first-floor apartment at 103 Lambeth Palace Road, not far from St. Thomas' Hospital. He'd lived in the same area during his previous stay in the city over a decade earlier and it hadn't changed much. Lambeth was still a slum of damp, narrow streets, run-down apartments, and meager industry. It still teemed with the destitute, the unemployed, and the down-at-heel. It still reeked of fish shops, hop yards, and unwashed humanity. And yet, there was no shortage of amusements, with a tavern seemingly on every corner, music halls like the Canterbury, Old Vic, and Gatti's, and plenty of entertainments of the flesh. This, of course, is what Dr. Thomas Neill Cream was most interested in.

The first unfortunate to encounter him was a pretty 19-year-old prostitute named Ellen "Nellie" Donworth. Nellie shared a room near Commercial Street with an army private named Ernest Linnell, who didn't seem to mind her occupation. At around six o'clock on the evening of October 13, she left her abode after telling a friend, Annie Clements, that she was going to meet a gentleman.

Later that evening, another friend, Constance Linfield, saw Nellie walking arm in arm with a "topper," (Victorian slang for a well-dressed gentleman in a top hat). Not long after, James Styles spotted Nellie alone, leaning on a gate on Morpeth Place. She was barely able to stand and Styles, at first, assumed that she was drunk. However, as he got closer, he saw that she was in severe pain. He helped her back to her lodging house and put her to bed, but by this time she was convulsing and grabbing her abdomen in agony. "That gentleman with the top hat gave me a drink out of a bottle with white stuff in it!" she moaned.

While Nellie's landlady remained with her, Styles ran to fetch an intern named Johnson from the nearby Lambeth Medical Institute. By the time they returned, Nellie's spasms were so severe that all of them together could not hold her down. The medic recognized her symptoms immediately as poisoning and instructed Styles to fetch a police officer. Nellie was then transported to St. Thomas' Hospital. She died before she got there.

A postmortem two days later found lethal doses of strychnine in Nellie Donworth's stomach. Coroner Thomas Herbert reported that the last several hours of her life must have been spent in extreme agony. Strychnine poisoning is a terrible way to die, characterized by extreme muscle convulsions and the feeling of being suffocated. In the final stages, the face turns blue and all of the muscles go rigid. Eventually the lungs contract to such an extent that the person dies from lack of oxygen, the face fixed in a macabre grin. Death can take anything from one to three hours. The person remains lucid throughout.

Cream bought his supplies of strychnine from Priest's Chemists, 22 Parliament Street. Because he was a certified doctor, he had no trouble getting what he wanted, although, by law, he was required to sign the poisons register. By following the entries in this journal, the police were later able to trace each of his deadly purchases.

Nellie Donworth had been given the poison in liquid form. For his next victim, Cream purchased a supply of gelatin capsules.

Twenty-seven-year-old Matilda Clover lived at 27 Lambeth Road with her two-year-old son, her landlord Mr. Vowles and his wife, and a servant girl, Lucy Rose. Matilda had turned to prostitution after her boy's father had deserted them. She also had an alcohol problem but had recently started visiting a doctor to cure that affliction.

On the night of October 20, Matilda left her room just after dark. Lucy saw her leave and presumed she was on her way to meet a man named Fred. Lucy only knew about Fred because she'd seen a note from him on Matilda's bedside table, asking her to meet him at the Canterbury.

At around 9 p.m. Matilda returned home in the company of a gentleman. Lucy got a good look at the man and would later describe him as tall and well dressed, in a cape and top hat. After leaving the man alone in her room, Matilda went out to buy some ale. A short while later the man left – alone.

At around 3 a.m., the entire house was woken by horrendous screams from Matilda's quarters. Lucy rushed to Matilda's room and was met there by the Vowles. As they entered, they saw Matilda lying naked on the bed, her body racked by convulsions. Contorted in pain, the woman screamed that Fred had given her some pills that had poisoned her. Lucy ran for a doctor, but it was too late. Matilda Clover died in agony at approximately seven in the morning.

Despite learning of Matilda's deathbed accusation against the mysterious "Fred," the doctor decided that she'd died due to mixing alcohol with a sedative she'd been prescribed. He recorded the cause of death as, "primarily, delirium tremens; secondly, syncope." It would be six months before the police realized that Matilda Clover was the second victim of the so-called, "Lambeth Poisoner."

In November 1881, a month after he killed Matilda Clover, Cream got a telegram from his family asking him to come home for the final disbursement of his father's property. He sailed from Liverpool aboard the SS Sernia on January 7, 1892, returning to Britain four months later. Not long after his return, Cream became engaged to the pretty and respectable Laura Sabbatini. But if the nefarious Dr. Cream was seriously thinking about settling down to matrimonial bliss, he had no plans just yet of giving up his nocturnal ramblings.

Roaming Piccadilly one day, he spotted an attractive young woman who he reckoned for a streetwalker. Approaching the woman, Cream introduced himself, told her he was a doctor from America and was currently practicing at St. Thomas' Hospital. He invited her to join him for dinner at the Palace Hotel and there learned that her name was Lou Harvey. Lou (real name Louise Harris) was a bright young woman and despite Cream's urbane manner, she was wary of him.

Nonetheless, when he invited her to meet him later for drinks and a show at the Oxford Music Hall, she agreed. They arranged to meet at 7:30 p.m. Before leaving, Cream told Lou that he'd bring her some pills that would bring some color to her cheeks.

Cream arrived for the rendezvous at the appointed time. He and Lou then walked from Charing Cross underground station to the Northumberland Public House. They had a glass of wine, before walking along the Embankment. There, Cream suddenly stopped and produced the two capsules he'd promised. Lou had already decided that she wasn't going to take them, but she pretended to put them in her mouth. Then, as Cream looked away, she tossed the capsules over the Embankment. Once he thought she'd taken the pills, Cream suddenly remembered a meeting at St. Thomas' Hospital and departed, giving the woman five shillings to go to the theater. He promised to meet her there at 11, but of course, he never showed.

On April 11, 1892, Cream met Alice Marsh, 21, and Emma Shrivell, 18, in St. George's Circus and arranged to go with the two prostitutes to their flat at 118 Stamford Street, Lambeth. There, the trio had a few drinks after which Cream promised to give them some pills that prevented venereal disease, every working girl's nightmare in an era when customers did not use condoms. Cream spent several hours with the women, leaving eventually at around 2 a.m. Outside, he encountered the local bobby, Officer Comley, and the two exchanged greetings before Cream disappeared into the night.

At around 2:30, Mrs. Charlotte Vogt, landlady at 118 Stamford, woke to the sound of screams. She quickly roused her husband and the pair hurried upstairs.

Alice Marsh lay in the hallway, her body wracked by spasms. From inside the room, Mr. Vogt heard a banging sound and found Emma Shrivell in similar agony, thrashing around, her body contorted into poses Mr. Vogt didn't think a human being was capable of, her foot slamming the wall as she fought for oxygen.

Vogt ran for a policeman, who, in turn, summoned an ambulance. But it was too late. The women were dead even before they reached St. Thomas'. An autopsy revealed deadly doses of strychnine, leading the police to link these deaths to that of Ellen Donworth, six months earlier.

The killer meanwhile, had concocted a plan whereby he might profit from his crimes. Money, of course, was not Thomas Neill Cream's primary motive. He enjoyed killing, of that there can be little doubt. However, he now initiated an ill-conceived blackmail scheme, directing extortion notices to a number of reputable London physicians, accusing them of committing the murders and offering to suppress the "evidence" he had – for a price. None of these eminent gentlemen took the bait and instead reported the extortion efforts to the police, something that would later come back to haunt Cream.

With the Metropolitan police having made the connection between the Donworth, Marsh, and Shrivell murders, they stepped up their hunt for the Lambeth Poisoner. Chemists' poisons registries were scoured for the names of known criminals, while the police hunted down and questioned any thug with a history of violence, especially violence towards women. When these efforts turned up no viable suspects they expanded their search beyond London. With the six-month gap between the murders (largely due to Cream's trip to Canada) the general belief among investigators was that the murderer was a maritime man who killed at his ports of call. This line of inquiry also led nowhere.

Like many serial killers, Dr. Cream's downfall was largely due to his own actions. He might have remained at liberty indefinitely, might even, like his hero Jack the Ripper, have escaped justice altogether. All he had to do was keep his mouth shut about the murders. But Cream couldn't keep his mouth shut, the world had to know of his genius.

In April 1892, a few days after the Stamford Street murders, Cream met a former New York City detective named John Haynes. The murders, having occurred just a few day's hence, were a hot topic of conversation and the two men got talking about them. Haynes was immediately impressed by Cream's knowledge on the subject, but somewhat confused when he mentioned two victims Haynes hadn't heard of - Matilda Clover and Lou Harvey.

After the two men had dinner together, Cream offered to walk Haynes through Lambeth and show him where the murders had been committed. The detective naturally agreed, but Cream showed him more than just the murder sites. Speaking in the third person, Cream related where he'd met each of his victims, where he'd taken them for drinks, where he'd passed his deadly prescriptions. It didn't take Harvey long to realize that what he was hearing was virtually a confession to the crimes.

The following day, Haynes took this information to his friend, Inspector Patrick McIntyre of Scotland Yard. McIntyre was intrigued by the story, in particular, Cream's mention of Matilda Clover. At this stage, Clover was still not considered a murder victim, but her name had been mentioned in one of the blackmail letters. As to the other name – Lou Harvey – McIntyre was as much in the dark as his friend. However, he made inquiries with the morgue, and when that turned up nothing, launched a search to find the woman.

Meanwhile, Cream was placed under surveillance while background checks were run which revealed his true identity (he'd introduced himself to Haynes as Dr. Neill). The police also learned that Cream had been convicted in America of murdering a man with strychnine. With this information in hand, McIntyre obtained an exhumation order for Matilda Clover. The subsequent autopsy turned up copious amounts of strychnine in her system.

The net that was closing around Cream drew ever closer when both Lucy Rose and PC Comley provided descriptions of the man they'd seen at the crime scenes. These closely matched Cream. And there was further evidence when a sample of Dr. Cream's handwriting was compared to the extortion letters and found to be a match.

Cream was arrested on June 3. The charge at this stage was not murder, but blackmail. However, the police wanted Cream off the streets while they built their murder case.

The inquest into Martha Clover's death began at Vestry Hall, Tooting on June 22. During the two-week hearing, a succession of witnesses stepped forward to build an ever-strengthening case against Cream. Still, the doctor seemed unfazed, even writing to his fiancé to tell her not to worry and to assure her that he'd been falsely accused and would soon be free.

Cream maintained his air of indifference throughout the first week of the proceedings and through most of the second. Then, on the penultimate day, a witness was introduced who caused his mask to slip. The police had finally succeeded in tracking down Lou Harvey. As she strode confidently forward, Cream did a double take, removed his spectacles, polished them, and then replaced them on his nose. It was as though he'd seen a ghost and to him, of course, Lou *was* a ghost. He was sure that he'd killed her.

Lou Harvey's testimony sealed Thomas Cream's fate. On July 13, the inquest concluded that Cream had administered strychnine to Matilda Clover, thereby causing her death. He was removed to

Newgate Prison, to await trial for murder. In subsequent weeks, he was also charged with premeditated homicide in the deaths of Nellie Donworth, Alice Marsh, and Emma Shrivell. A charge of attempted murder was added for Lou Harvey, and there were also charges of blackmail to answer.

The trial of Dr. Thomas Neill Cream took place over a five-day period from October 17 to 21, Justice Henry Hawkins presiding. The prosecution produced pretty much the same line-up of witnesses they'd called at the inquest while the defense produced none, their strategy focused on discrediting the evidence as circumstantial. It was never likely to succeed. The jury took just 10 minutes of deliberation before pronouncing Cream guilty.

Cream went to the gallows on November 16, 1892. But he would not go quietly to his grave. In the moment just before the trapdoor was sprung, he shouted from under the hood, "I am Jack –". The rest of the phrase was extinguished as he plunged to his death. Over a century later, debate still rages as to what Cream meant to say, the consensus being that he intended identifying himself as Jack the Ripper.

On the face of it, Cream makes a compelling Ripper suspect. Quite clearly, he had a pathological hatred of women in general, and prostitutes in particular. He also had a medical background – something that most Ripper experts believe was true of Jack. And although he was slightly taller than the man spotted with some of the Ripper victims, he resembled him in other respects.

So, was Dr. Thomas Neill Cream the elusive Jack? Unfortunately for those who seek an answer to the mystery, he was not. The Ripper murders took place in 1888, at which time Cream was serving a life sentence at Joliet, on the other side of the Atlantic.

For more True Crime books by Robert Keller please visit

http://bit.ly/kellerbooks

Made in the USA
Columbia, SC
16 November 2019

83107006R00089